EARLY PRAISE FOR *PREYED UPON*

Rosaline Alam is more than courageous. She is a fighter, a survivor and a thriver! She has risen above all of the trauma and darkness life sunk her into and sprouted as high as the angels above. *Preyed Upon* is a testimony that will pull every woman from the soils of their own tragedy and lift them into light. It's a must-read.

—Tammi Mac
Actress, Radio/TV Host

Preyed Upon is a heart wrenching and thought-provoking book that you will not be able to put down! It is an important reminder that we need to be careful who we allow our kids to be around because predators can be family members and people, we think are friends. It's clear that the author put her pain aside to be able to tell her story to help other parents who are dealing with similar situations. It's also a beautiful love letter to her children because it's evident in her writing that her children have and will always be the most important part of her life. I recommend this book to everyone whether you have children or not because there are so many nuggets of wisdom in each chapter that we can all apply to our lives.

—Elvira Guzman-Barnett

PREYED UPON

PREYED UPON

MULTIPLE GENERATIONS OF PARENTAL ALIENATION

ROSALINE ALAM

PALMETTO
PUBLISHING
Charleston, SC
www.PalmettoPublishing.com

Hardcover ISBN: 979-8-8229-5366-6
Paperback ISBN: 979-8-8229-2148-1
eBook ISBN: 979-8-8229-2149-8

AUTHOR'S NOTE

This book is a memoir. It reflects my present recollections of experiences over time. Names, characteristics, and locations have been changed, some events have been compressed, and some dialogue has been recreated.

DEDICATION

To Jazoul and Richie Rich, never be scared to do what's right. I love you forever; our bond is everlasting.

FOREWORD

"Preyed Upon" is a unique book that not only touches your heart but awakens your spirit.

In this book Rosaline powerfully shares her story and the reader quickly immerses in it. You feel like you are beside her rooting her on!

Sadly, Rosaline's story of being preyed upon and then groomed by her father's friend, a man 19 years her senior is far too common. Having her innocence and virginity taken away from her is something a child should never have to experience.

Being taken away from her parents, not being allowed to see them or speak to them is simply heartbreaking. Especially for a young girl from a different country.

This book is a wakeup call that parental alienation must be penalized or the generations to follow will continue to suffer and the cycles of abuse will never end. It's very clear in Rosaline's case that the people who are suffering the most are her children who have been mentally manipulated and abused just as she was.

It's disheartening to know that the legal system has no way of stopping this type of abuse from predators and manipulative parents.

The repercussions of parental alienation are detrimental to the future of the children and yet there is nothing Rosaline and many other parents in the same situation can do.

In this book Rosaline gives incredible tips on how to survive dealing with a situation like hers. She beautifully explains that self-care and having a purpose is important to overcome the overwhelming feelings that come from being rejected by your children.

Rosalin's story will not only inspire you, it will show you that while doing all you can to get your children back, having a successful and joyful life is possible! She fearlessly explains that we must be kind to ourselves so that when our children return, they will see a woman they are proud to call their mom. She vigorously demonstrates the power in forgiveness in order to move forward for the sake of her children.

"Preyed Upon" is a phenomenal book that shows the depth of a parent's love and is a beautiful reminder of what true love really is.

Rosaline is an incredible mother and a survivor. She dug deep into her soul to write this book and to help as many people as possible overcome those difficult moments so that we can keep going and never give up!

I pray her words and wisdom fill the parts of you that need hope and that one day you will be reunited with your children. Children are the beat of a parent's heart.

Nautica de la Cruz
Radio Host & Entrepreneur

TABLE OF CONTENTS

CHAPTER 1

A Mother's Plea

The only thing necessary for the triumph
of evil is for good men to do nothing.
—Edmund Burke

In the Cathedral of Our Lady of Angels, I sit below the Mother of God and pray that my children will come home. You know my struggle, I say to her, the Blessed Mary.

She, too, had her child taken from her, so it is to her I beg.

Religion has always been tough for me, so I've stayed at arm's length, but I know the devil when I see him. He has followed me to America from Syria. He stole my innocence. And then stole my kids.

"Please," I say to Mary. "Both of my children have been seduced by evil, ripped from my arms, and there's not a thing I can do to bring them home but pray. So here I sit, and here I pray. Please return my children."

Years after seducing me at the age of sixteen, when he was thirty-five, my now ex-husband is preying upon our two children, convincing them that I am a bad mother, that I am the devil. But that's exactly what the devil does—he points his finger at others so he can hide in the shadows. And unfortunately, my kids believe it, and the American legal system can't do anything about it. My kids were convinced at a young age that I don't truly love them, but all I can do is love. Each day I pray that they will return home to me. Each day I pray that they will be unchained from the devil. Each day I beg God.

But this isn't just a mother begging.

This isn't just a mother's prayer.

This isn't just a mother's plea for her children to come home.

This is a warning.

My family and I arrived in Chicago on a cold morning in 1985—all of our belongings in a few suitcases—unaware that *al shaytan*, Arabic for the devil, would soon follow.

The American dream. That's what my dad called it. The Muslim Brotherhood uprising in Syria was getting worse, and he knew we needed to get out. The plan was for our father to lead us to America and earn some money so he could provide for our family. He was a skilled jeweler in Syria, so he could do just as well, if not better, in America. A better life for our family was his ultimate goal.

But no matter how far away we went, everything was still the same. Family was still the same. Our relationships were still the same. I'm not sure what I expected to happen when we moved to America—maybe I thought everything would be different, including our relationships, but nothing was. Our lives certainly changed—the way we interacted in the world, the way the world interacted with us. We were Syrians trying to adapt, but at the end of the day, we could never stop being Syrians.

Americans seemed to be very affectionate and aware of each other's space. Syrians couldn't be more different. There wasn't a lot of affection growing up, especially from my parents. That might sound like a bad thing, but it really isn't; it's just the way things are. To Syrians, that's normal. You really didn't see a lot of hugging or kissing. Affection was expressed in the form of asking if I had any homework or how my day was going and providing for us.

<hr>

We landed in Chicago, but we didn't stay long—two years, to be exact—before we headed west to California. But acclimation to the American culture proved more difficult than one would imagine. It's almost funny how seamless the American dream appears to be. I mean, when you think about it, it sounds like a thrill. You move to a new country, start a new life, and live happily ever after. What they don't tell you is that the American dream is only seamless if you want to truly be engulfed in American culture. If you don't accept the imposition the culture makes on you, it can be jarring. It can be like putting a square peg in a round hole, for lack of a better expression.

Socially, my parents were fine because we lived near other Arabs and Middle Easterners. It's tough for a foreigner to move into an all-American neighborhood because then they are the outsider. If he moves into an all-Arab community, he suddenly becomes a neighbor. You can't blame a square peg for naturally wanting to fit into the square hole; therefore my parents had little desire to fit into that round hole. They had their own idea of the American dream, and it made them happy.

And that dream, of course, imprinted on their square-peg children. You can take the family out of Syria, but you can't take the Syrian out of the family. Back in the day, Syrian women weren't really allowed to have dreams. It was part of the culture. Thankfully, things have changed, and women are now allowed (and expected) to make something of themselves, but sometimes the ghost of our past still lingers.

One by one, a lot of our family and friends followed us to America. My grandmother Audelia lived with us after my grandfather died. Every time I think back about her life, I get sad. She had nothing to live for other than her family. She never drove. She never worked an actual job. She never had a passion. She raised her grandkids, cooked and cleaned, and went to sleep at night. The thing is, though, that no one told her she had to do any of these things. It was simply what she thought she had to do, just as many Syrian women are taught.

Back in Syria, she lived deep in this culture, working in the fields and tending to the house. Even when she was pregnant with her five kids, she could be found working the fields. And when she had the baby, it was right back out to the fields. Deep down, I think I always knew that I wanted a different life, that I wanted my life to be more than that. In Syria, there's sort of a "when you die, you die" attitude. Meaning, your responsibility in life is to take care of your family and simply to exist. Bettering one's life isn't common because one was confined to their surroundings. They wanted to be better, to live better, but that usually consisted of getting a better house, not moving to a new country. In a way, there really wasn't a lot of curiosity about what other people were doing around the world. The young men did think about what it would be like to go to another country and a lot of them did, and still do, try to leave to find a better financial future for their family. However, leaving Syria is not easy when politics is involved. It is very hard to get a visa to travel outside of Syria. In the 1980's it was easier than it is now as long as you had a sponsor from the United States. The young Syrian women did not have the luxury of trying to leave for a better future. If they did leave it was either with their immediate family or if they were married. The thought of sending a young women by herself to another country was unheard of! Now, it is accepted and it does happen but usually it is to continue their education. When my parents and family moved to the States, a fire sparked deep within me, deeper than consciously possible. I was just a child, yet the fire was there.

After my grandfather died, my grandmother moved in with my parents. In Syria, when a woman's husband dies, she becomes a widow for life, forbidden to remarry. Once again—there is no hard-and-fast rule that says they cannot; it's simply the way they are taught to live. If a husband's wife died during childbirth, though, forget about it. It wasn't uncommon for the man to be remarried within a few months. These days, things are much looser, but back then, culture was life and culture was death.

It's that old Syrian culture that perpetuated the actions that led to my children being taken away. But can a culture be labeled as "wrong?" Who is the judge and jury deciding this verdict? Maybe that's the reason it lasted so long.

Grandma died a few years ago after a hundred years of existing, and I'm grateful that she lived long enough to realize that a woman can be just as powerful, if not more powerful, than a man. I credit her and my mom for my courage, for my strength. She held back so I could move forward.

One evening in 1987, in our little Arcadia apartment, I heard an unknown male voice in the living room, so I rushed out to see who it was. Although visitors weren't rare, they were still cause for excitement.

The gentleman hugged my mom, then noticed me in the doorway. He had charcoal-black hair, and his collared shirt tucked into his jeans made him look even taller than he was. His mustache—the typical eighties chevron 'stache—was thick and complemented the aviators hanging from his shirt.

"Well, look at you," he said with a grin on his face. "My Maia certainly has grown."

I didn't remember Adder, but my parents said he was their old friend from Syria who would often come over to the house. I was only seven, so the thought of me growing just sounded silly. But he was an adult, and he seemed to know better than I did. The thing about Syrian households is that everyone is welcome, always. Friends, family, neighbors—there is always someone around or someone dropping by. Another quality of Syrian households is that the adults don't really interact with the children that much. There are playful jokes exchanged and minor conversations, but for the most part, children are left to play with the other children.

That first night that Adder came over, we played hide-and-go-seek. As we got older, it was exciting when other people came over because we would be allowed to stay up late, play games, play cards. And back then, I thought he played games with us simply to appease us kids. But he didn't. He seemed to genuinely care about us, about me. Even when I was bullied at school for how I was dressed or for my unibrow, Adder never mentioned it. He seemed to care about the good things and not care about the things I thought were bad.

When I look back at pictures of myself in school, I can't believe I ever left the house looking like that—the weird hairdos that tried so hard to fit into the eighties, nearly looking like a parody, the clothes that fit perfectly yet looked like they belonged to a kindergartener, the unibrow and the hairy arms. What I would have given for the modern-day convenience of YouTube tutorials or Pinterest boards. But instead, they bullied me. They made fun of me. They called me Chewbacca. But I always knew that my family, including Adder, still loved me and that I was going to be OK.

Nevertheless, in the eighth grade, I started to steal my mom's makeup to try to ease the pain. I would shove it in my backpack and rush off to school. Sometimes I could only get my sticky fingers on the powder, sometimes just the mascara. On a good day, I got enough to complete the face. I'd rush into the bathroom as soon as I got to school and apply whatever I had, and the bullying would be much easier that day. And right before I'd go out the door to get in my mom's car, I'd wash my face in the bathroom.

One day, as I was about to leave school, I realized I had forgotten to take my makeup off. I had gotten too comfortable. I begged the teacher to let me go to the bathroom. She sighed, giving me that "Are you kidding me?" look.

"Quickly," she said, almost as if she was going to change her mind. I speed-walked to the bathroom, washed off, then ran right back. When we got home, I walked through the front door of our house more than confident. I couldn't believe I had gotten away with it again. It was a thrill pretending to be like one of my American-born friends, to be more than they thought I was. My mom asked me how my day was, and just as she turned the corner in the kitchen, she said, "Come here."

You know nothing, I thought, so confidently. It was almost devious the way I was so confident in my disposal of the evidence. She took a Kleenex off the counter and wiped the side of my face.

"What is this?" she asked.

Aw, shit, I thought. She washed my face, removing any remnants of my double-side, my alter ego, my cool girl.

Wearing makeup—it never seems like that big of a deal to most people. And oddly, in that same breath, not wearing makeup is also not a big deal for most people. Not doing your eyebrows, not shaving your arms and legs—it's all so innocent, one might think. But for me, it was the difference in self-esteem and confidence. I stood out, and I paid the price for it. At school, if I was makeup less and full-eyebrow bush, the boys would point and laugh. They would call me Unibrow. And when Mom took away my makeup, I was forced to go back to my real self.

Finally, in high school, I was allowed to be reintroduced to my alter ego, the cleaner, fresher version of myself. My mom was reluctant, but still, her friend took me to get my unibrow plucked. I understand the resistance, though—the fear that, by going against the Syrian culture of keeping women unsexualized, she would lose me to America, she would lose me to boys, she would lose me. A woman trying to align herself with modern beauty standards was, in a way, seen as the woman attempting to get attention that she shouldn't be getting. If you're unmarried, it is seen as promiscuous and tarnishing to your virginity. If you are married, it's seen as you trying to throw yourself at other men.

Now, granted, they didn't shape my eyebrows when my mom's friend took me; they just got rid of the unibrow. Shit, I thought. I'll take what I can get.

I will say that it isn't just Syrian culture that prohibits women from doing many things, including trying to adhere to beauty standards. In Mexican culture, girls often aren't allowed to shave their legs until a certain age because that means that they're trying to get a boyfriend or be promiscuous. Thankfully my mom let me wax my legs at a certain point, allowing me to avoid the "Hairiest Girl" award. And yes, wax, not shave. My mom said that if I wanted to get rid of the hair, I was going to have to go through the pain of waxing. I'm still not sure of her reason, but I figured if I could avoid looking like an animal, I'd take the pain any day.

It's funny because it's pain that most Syrians try to protect each other from. We all try to protect ourselves and each other from the pain and the shame, to protect our family names. Women can't practice modern beauty lest they be seen as promiscuous. Children can't know about sex lest they be exposed early on and lose their innocence. Women can't work lest they become more powerful than the man of the house—which, in Syrian culture, is considered inappropriate. In Syrian culture, there is a formula, an expectation, for how everyone should behave. Deviate from that, and shame can be brought to your entire family's name. It's this thinking, this fear, that keeps that control in play. It wasn't until I was older that I realized how much making decisions based on fear impacted my life.

When I turned thirteen, the family was out standing in the driveway of my parents' house. We were greeting friends who had just arrived, including Adder, and chitchatting about anything and everything. It was a classic Syrian greeting. The California sun was warm on my shoulders as I wore a black tank top and shorts. I was excited that there were people over at the house and that the weather was gorgeous.

Adder stood towering over his car, dressed in jeans and a short-sleeved polo shirt. He strutted forward, zeroing in on me, and said, "Come here, Maia. Let me give you a hug."

He was a family friend, basically family. I said OK innocently. We always hugged. He knelt and wrapped his arms around me, and I reciprocated. When I went to pull away, his grip held tight, one hand rubbing my back. I pushed a little harder, trying to signal that I was done, but his grip got even tighter. This is weird, I thought, not sure why he wouldn't let go. Finally, I pushed hard enough to break free, looking up only for a moment to notice a grin on his face, as if he had just won something. I turned to go inside, to get away from the awkward encounter.

"Where are you going?" he asked.

"I have to go inside," I said, rushing in.

I'm not sure what changed, but suddenly Adder's friendliness wasn't fun anymore. It scared me. It made me want to repent, as I knew it was wrong. And these feelings continued because his behavior never stopped. The way he would go out of his way to be with us—to be with me, in particular—didn't feel right. When he would hug me, there was a different energy, almost as if his intentions had changed. When he would roughhouse with me, I would ask him to stop, and when he finally would, I'd find my parents and stay by their side for the rest of his visit. When he would pat me on the shoulder or tell me I looked good, it made my heart race. Not in the excited, fluttery way I would later feel with other boys—boys my age, to be clear—but rather in an uncomfortable way that made me want to run and hide. I knew that something had changed and that his presence was no longer safe, but as a kid, I just couldn't explain it. All I knew was that it was wrong.

Syrian parents never really show affection to each other, at least in front of their children. Who knows what they do behind closed doors, but in the company of others, it's pretty mild. My parents have been married for more than forty years, and I can say that for at least my entire life, they've been this way. When Adder would touch me, it was this new and confusing experience. Why would he do this? I'd ask myself. No matter the reason, and no matter whether I could identify it as this or not, I knew it was inappropriate and that I wanted it to stop.

I started trying to avoid him. If we all went to the park as a family, I made sure to walk out the door first so I would be in my parents' view. If we were all sitting outside, I made sure never to go into the house alone, lest he follow me in. If we were in the same room, I'd start to sweat because I knew that what was happening was wrong, and I thought if my parents found out, I would be the one to get in trouble. It was the same type of fear that we tried to protect each other from that would set in around him, and I thought I couldn't tell a soul.

Fear—it was taboo. If the family was watching television and there was a sex scene, my parents would freak out and turn the TV off. Even if it was as innocent as a kissing scene, the channel would be switched. The innocence had to be protected at all costs. I wasn't even allowed to have a friend who was a guy out of fear that it would turn romantic. If I wanted to call a guy friend and chitchat or go to the movies, I had to suppress that desire because I knew my parents would be ashamed. I couldn't even have a sleepover at a friend's house. In this American dream, I was limited to the laws of our Syrian culture, left to be teased by the Americanism around me. All these rules were meant to protect me from the unknown, the outside world. Little did my parents know that I needed protection within my own home.

The torture ran even deeper as in Syrian culture, we didn't talk about all of the things we weren't allowed to do or anything that was even remotely related. Even in school I wasn't allowed to watch the sex education videos. My parents would take me out of school that day, so I never really knew about how my body would change. Well, I didn't even know that my body would change, so when it did, I was shocked, scared. Maybe it was just their way of protecting me, but in a way, it did more harm than good, especially given that when I got my period for the first time, I thought I was dying. I was scared and confused. No one ever prepared me for that moment, and I certainly believed I wasn't allowed to ask. When I woke up with blood-soaked underwear, I shoved them in a drawer because I had no clue what was going on. I thought my mom would find the blood and get worried.

My aunt, my mom's sister, was living with us at the time. I don't know if she saw me hiding the underwear or if she was snooping or what happened, but either way, my aunt found the underwear and told my mom. Finally my mom gave me a talk about it—quite literally the basics and as little as she could get away with telling me—but that was it, period.

If only avoiding Adder had been as easy as shoving bloody underwear in a drawer. Avoiding him took a lot of calculating, a lot of manipulating, which was a lot for a thirteen-year-old girl. What shocked me most, though, was how he had so ingrained himself in my family that his actions went unnoticed. They trusted him. They did their jobs as parents, and they did them well. Why should they have suspected anything? Right in front of them, he would make comments like, "Oh, you're looking good" or "Those shorts look great on you, Maia." These seeming compliments were, in retrospect, sexual advances, but who would expect a man nineteen years older than an underage girl to behave that way, to treat an underage girl that way? In a way, I don't blame my parents for not noticing.

And every move I'd make, he would notice. I could feel his eyes on me, watching me.

CHAPTER 2

His Eyes

*You never know how strong you are, until
being strong is your only choice.*
—Bob Marley

When I was sixteen, I breathed a great sigh of relief when
Adder got married to a woman—twelve years younger than
him, yet still of legal age, unlike I was at the time.

She was a gorgeous bride and invited me to be one of her
bridesmaids. We rode in the limo to the church in Los Angeles
in our burgundy dresses with our hair done up nice. I felt like
a princess. There was ecstatic emotion radiating off of me. I
knew I was happy, joyful, grateful even, but I didn't realize
then that it wasn't because I was happy for the couple; it was
because I was happy for myself.

It was a typical Syrian wedding, with big drums that everyone could bang on. Everyone was merry and effervescent.
This family member we all knew and some loved was going to
spend the rest of his life with this gorgeous woman. There was
dancing and drinking, ties being loosened, bouquets being
thrown. The only way in which the wedding diverged from a

typical Syrian wedding was that there were probably only one hundred people there. Recently my cousin got married and there had to have been at least six hundred people in attendance. Now that is a Syrian wedding!

Over the next two weeks, we visited the lucky couple at their house for barbecues and whatnot. We celebrated them, and they seemed happy. They would come over to our house on occasion, but I was safe at these times. He stayed with his wife for the duration of the visits, and I was free. I don't know much about their relationship or much about her, but what I do know is that she was smart. She was Middle Eastern, just like we were, but she had grown up in America, so she knew how to own her voice. In a way, I was jealous of her for that. In a way, I was sad for her for marrying him, but I was happier for myself for not being in her shoes.

At sixteen, I felt true freedom for the first time. After years of being watched, after years of being touched, I was allowed to be a kid again.

But it was her intelligence that brought that freedom to an end. Only one month after their nuptials, she left him, and their marriage was annulled. Ah, shit, I thought. My mom said that she knew the marriage wouldn't last because he was controlling, only after his own agenda. And why should she stay with him, given the way he treats her? she would say. If only my mother knew that would be my fate too.

Within a few weeks, he was back over at our house just like before. He was back to watching me. His eyes followed me more intently now. He started asking me about boys, asking me if I liked anyone. At first I thought they were trick questions because I knew I wasn't supposed to be interested in boys, but then again, didn't he do and say every inappropriate thing behind my parents' backs? He knew this sort of thing wasn't allowed because he knew *our* culture. He had spent more time in Syria than I had. He knew that kids wanted to talk about this sort of thing but they never could in front of adults. Suddenly, he was trying to be one of us kids, trying to gain my trust. And I fell for it.

I talked with him about boys. I talked with him about my body. I talked with him about sex. After a few conversations like this, that same uncomfortable feeling came back—the one I had gotten years before when he would touch me, when he would stare at me, when he would hug me. And suddenly, I felt the wave of fear and guilt. I knew I shouldn't have been talking about that sort of thing. Deep down, I knew. But there I was, needing to say more because if I didn't, he'd pry, not in a kind and fun way but in a threatening way. And I didn't have the voice to stand up for myself. I simply wasn't powerful enough.

About a month after his annulment, he called me on the phone at my house. I was the only person home, and my parents had told him since they always shared their plans with their friends and family. He knew they were planning a trip, so he told me to stay home, to do whatever I could to stay home because he wanted to talk with me on the phone. I didn't go. I stayed home. I was afraid of what would happen if I didn't. I waited, my heart racing, for the phone to ring. With each passing moment, I knew it would ring, but when it did, my heart must have stopped, shooting fear through all parts of my body. We exchanged pleasantries, then he paused.

"Go stand in front of the mirror," he requested. I did as I was told.

"Tell me," he said, "what you don't like about your body."

Shame manifested in the form of beads of sweat on my forehead. My hand shook as I held the receiver. "Well, you know, I guess I don't like my butt." He told me to turn sideways and look in the mirror. I did.

"Touch your butt. See? See how it curves?"

"Yeah," I whispered.

"That means that you have a really nice butt," he said. "Keep feeling it. Touch it, and feel the curves."

I did.

There was a creak in the hallway, and I fumbled the receiver, shoving it out of sight. It had to have been my parents, I thought, but how? They were gone and not expected back until late in the night. This is how it ends. They're going to kill me. Fuck.

I wiped my forehead, rushing for the door.

Nobody. Must have just been the old house.

I went back to the phone and apologized.

"It's OK," he said.

"See those curves again?"

"Yeah," I said.

"Put your hand on them, and slowly move your hand back up your side. See how those curves move upward?"

"Yeah."

"Where do they lead?"

"My breasts."

There was a pause, a light yet labored breathing from the other end.

The sweat on my forehead returned.

"Do you hate your boobs?" he asked.

"A little," I said.

"Put your palms over them. Do your palms cover them?"

"No,"

"Then that means they're not small. You should like them. I do."

The anxiety in my body turned to guilt. I couldn't keep up with my thoughts during the call and after, and in those moments, I couldn't process what had just happened to me.

"Don't tell anyone," he said at the end of the call. "I mean it. You know that we can't be doing this. If your parents find out…" He paused. "They could…" He didn't even have to finish the sentence. I knew exactly what they could do. Women were killed for things like this back in Syria. I knew exactly what this meant because he had planted that in my head a while back. I knew what my fate could be.

In Syria (and many other countries across the world) honor killings are a cultural reality. Sometimes when I meet Americans and tell them about this, they think it's an ancient practice, but it's common and still occurs today. In essence, the honor killing is used when a family member has "brought shame unto the family." If this is done—typically it is a woman who brings the shame, but men have been known to do it, too, especially if they're gay—then the family members are within their rights to kill the offender in order to preserve the family's honor.

And there I was, a sixteen-year-old girl, bringing shame to my family. Culturally, you do what someone older tells you to do. That notion is instilled in Syrian children at a very young age. I'm sure my parents didn't mean for that notion to be taken that far, but I was young, naïve, and scared. I thought that I was not to question an elder out of basic respect, but in retrospect, that's not how the cultural proxy was intended. I had no clue what to do in that situation.

After the call, I sat on my bed, just staring at the wall. The shame took over, and I went into what seemed to be a trance. What the fuck just happened, I thought. Finally, what seemed like hours later, I tapped back into my thoughts as the shame turned to fear. Is he going to tell my parents? Is he going to come over here? What is going to happen, I wondered.

And that's exactly what Adder did best—instilled fear; he focused on my weak characteristics and traits in order to manipulate me. He knew that I would be crushed if my parents were disappointed with me, so he led me to believe they would be if I ever spoke up.

I thought about praying but that wouldn't have saved me from an honor killing if my parents found out. He instilled that fear in me in order to manipulate me, and it traumatized me. I thought about running away, but just how far could a sixteen-year-old girl run before they found me?

Eventually, my parents came home, Adder continued to come around, and although I lived in a state of fear, I knew that my parents didn't know, and I could continue to live. For now. As I look back, I think about my state of mind then and am in shock at how I believed that was possible, how I truly believed that my sweet, loving parents could ever do such a thing.

———◆———

About a week after the phone incident, the pace of our relationship—if you can call what this was a relationship—picked up, and slowly I started to realize the reasons why it was not OK.

I was terrible at math back then, and he knew it. One evening when he was over for a barbecue, he pulled me aside without my parents noticing and told me that, in a few minutes,

I was to call him into my room and ask for his help with my math. The fear that was already instilled in me intensified. I did as I was told.

When he entered my room, he pushed the door closed, leaving it just ever so slightly open—a crack to avoid suspicion from setting in.

"OK," he said, as if others could hear him, "what did you need help with?" He motioned for me to sit down at my desk.

I made up a problem and pointed to my book while his hand appeared on my shoulder. He agreed that it was quite the problem and slipped his hand down my shirt. His hand cupping my breast, I started to shiver. My heart started to race, and I wanted to leave. I wanted to back the chair into him and run out of the room. If my parents asked me where I was going, I'd just keep running. They couldn't know what had happened. I'd run out of the house, down the street, and disappear into the Arcadia sunset. But that's not how it happened. That's never how it happens. My body froze, and I could barely speak. Why, why did my body freeze? Why couldn't I stand up for myself?

Eventually it stopped—too much time in my room and either my parents would know what he was up to or they'd think I was really, truly terrible at math and put me in tutoring. I ran out to sit by my parents, determined to not be alone for the rest of the night. No way was he going to do it again. I hadn't been able to fight back then, but this time, I'll be damned if I wasn't going to fight. My parents were in the kitchen helping my grandma, and before I could get out to them, he asked me—loud enough so everyone heard—to sit outside with him, saying he wanted to show me something.

We had a patio, and the sofa was directly underneath the kitchen window where my family was cooking. Trembling, I followed. We sat on the couch, and he opened up his computer to porn! I panicked and tried to close it, fumbling for the laptop. This was the first time I had seen anything sexual.

"Turn it off," I shouted yet simultaneously whispered. "Everyone is going to see!"

"They'll never know," he said. "Look at them." He motioned up to the window with his head. "They have no idea. Just be quiet and watch."

And he was right. I looked up to the window, I tried so hard to scream, but nothing came out. I tried to scream with my eyes, to alert them. Didn't they say that you could always feel when someone was looking at you? Maybe, just maybe, if I looked hard enough…

There was a thrill in Adder's eyes and shit in his grin. He was manipulating me and in the process, taking advantage of my parents. He put his hand on my neck and turned my head back to the computer. I could feel his glee, but to me, it felt like torture.

"Do not ever," he said, looking into my eyes, "ever tell a soul."

He said it with a whisper, yet it felt like a million needles penetrating my body. It shook me to my core and struck me like the fear of God—instead it was the fear of Adder, which somehow was worse.

When you're forced into a corner with no way out, especially when you're a child and the person forcing you into a corner is an adult, there's a shift that occurs in your brain. It's almost as if you manipulate yourself into not feeling anything. I continued to have problems with my math homework, he continued to have things to show me on his laptop outside, and my parents continued to cook dinner, hovering above the kitchen window with absolutely no clue what was going on.

This is the way my life is going to be, I'd think. The math homework became the least of my worries as I accepted the fact that I had no choice but to submit. Why fight it? I'd ask myself. My mantra became "Just survive." If I could just survive this homework session, if I could just survive this outdoor porn viewing, I could make it to the next day. And I could make it to the day after that, and the day after that. I could live to see all of the days if I just existed instead of lived.

The time finally came to apply to colleges. It was weird being one of the first females in my family to have the opportunity to embark on a future all my own. I was excited. Maybe, just maybe, if I played my cards right, I could go off to college and never hear from Adder again.

One day after school, my mom was to pick me up to go look at colleges in the area. For whatever reason, she couldn't come, so she got Adder to go instead. I doubt it was her idea. Instead, I guarantee, he planted that seed in her head, that he was available and ready to take me on a tour, and who better than the guy who has always expressed great interest in your daughter?

We went to quite a few different schools, touring and interviewing. He told my parents about how he went to the University of California, Irvine, and what a fine school it was. He had connections, he told them, so it would be a great idea to at least send me on an interview. What could it hurt?

Of course, he took me to the interview and tour. Before the interview he told me that I needed to attend UC Irvine, that if I didn't, *he* would be extremely disappointed.

"Well, not just me. I mean, think of your family," he said. "At UC Irvine, I have connections. Your family will be so disappointed if you don't get into college, so you might as well take the chance."

Making me feel like I was not smart enough was a skill he had mastered. I mean, how could I doubt myself with a 3.6 GPA? Connections? What connections? I was accepted based on my own hard work.

After the interview he drove us in his little red Civic to his apartment. He had been more handsy with me than he had been before, so I guess in a sense, I knew what was coming. I asked him where we were going, and he said his place so we could "have some privacy."

"I really think we should get home," I suggested. "What if my parents notice we've been gone too long?"

"Oh please," he said, "they'll think we're still at the interview."

He pulled into the driveway and walked us in.

"You know, you're going to be in college soon. You're going to be an adult. And if you want to be an adult, you need to behave like one."

At that point my mind started to fade. I was there, but I wasn't. I was in survival mode, trying to comprehend what was about to happen. I had never had sex before, but I knew it was going to hurt.

We entered his bedroom, and it was obvious that he had prepared for this moment. There were pillows on the floor, strategically placed, as if to tell me the floor was more romantic. As if to tell me any part of this was romantic.

He laid me down on the pillows and took off his belt.

After we were done, we didn't linger too long. I was anxious, not really sure how to react. It was a state of panic, of feeling not in control. I had been used, and I had no say in the matter. If I spoke up and told someone, I could be killed. If I told him no, he would tell everyone that I wasn't honorable anymore. What would my dad do if he found out? Not only could he kill me, but he would also kill Adder. If they ever knew what was really happening…

Adder was thrilled after it ended. "You just had sex for the first time," he said, trying to pump me up. "It's this amazing thing! You should be so happy."

But I wasn't. I was stone-cold. I just wanted to go home.

"They're going to start to wonder," I told him. "I want to go home."

So he took me home.

When we got home, I went to my room to clean up. I wanted to cleanse my body, to purge my soul. I wanted to pray, to ask for forgiveness, even though I knew it wasn't my fault. I wanted to do anything I could think of to take that experience away.

I stayed in my bedroom as much as possible because I knew what had just happened to me, and the shame made me believe that my parents would be able to tell the difference. I thought they would notice something different about me; even if it was not a logical observation, it would be a sixth sense, I thought. Parents are good like that. I thought I was under the microscope, and in my bedroom, I could hide my fear and shame. I knew I was going to get caught, but I wasn't going to go into the dark night easily.

How could I look them in the eyes and pretend as if I hadn't just gone through one of the worst experiences of my life? And to make it worse, Adder came home with me. He sat in front of them and pretended as if nothing had happened, pretended to be their best friend, pretended as if he hadn't just raped their seventeen-year-old daughter.

I had always hoped that going away to college would be a liberating experience. I hoped that I would feel free, that I would be on my own for the first time, that I would be an adult. When I was accepted to UC Irvine, I was still in a forced relationship with Adder and it was determined that I would live at home with my parents, yet I still hoped that somehow things would have changed by the time I walked onto campus for my very first class. Maybe, suddenly, my parents would be hipper and let me live on campus, out of their home. Maybe Adder would suddenly lose interest in me and forget all about me. All of these thoughts were so silly. I'm not sure how I thought any of it was possible, because it clearly wasn't. I guess I just thought that one day I would wake up and everything would be different.

Instead, I woke up and my life was exactly the same. There I was, a freshman in college, living with my parents and stuck in a forced relationship with a man nineteen years older than me. I had always imagined a college life with tons of parties, hanging out in coffee houses, and late nights studying. Instead, I stayed home. And when I wasn't home, I was at Adder's. I wasn't allowed to join a sorority. I wasn't allowed to go to parties. I went to class, did my work, dealt with the demanding relationship, and then went home to deal with my parents. And the next day, I'd repeat. There was no socializing, no hanging out at school, no fun, no enjoying campus. I never made friends, other than the ones I had from middle and high school, because the demanding factors in my life were just too much.

Adder kept me on a schedule. He asked me to check in with him multiple times a day but always on a pay phone to make it even more inconspicuous. When he would instruct me to call him from my parents' house, we wouldn't talk very long because he knew that if my dad saw the length of time and the number on the phone bill, he'd know something was going on. Even when Adder would find different numbers to use—pay phones, office phones, friends' phones—we would keep it short, just long enough that he could check in on me and log my location.

Because I was driving more, and because I had classes at random buildings and times, Adder would concoct plans to allow me to get away from my parents more. From my parents' point of view, I had a lot of group projects in college, but in reality, I had maybe one or two. Nearly every time I finished a class, I took the road to Adder's house to spend time with him.

We were effectively a couple, even though I was eighteen when I first entered college. When I read books and watched movies, I saw how in love girls were with their boyfriends. The way they expressed themselves, the way they wrote letters and talked on the phone, the way they said they got butterflies in their stomachs—I wanted that, but I didn't want it with Adder. There was a mask of love that we wore—or at least that I wore—but it was just that: a mask. It never felt like love. It felt like that was how he wanted me to feel.

One day after class, I drove over to his house and he raved about love letters and how I didn't send him enough love letters. Enough? I thought. I don't send you any. But of course, I deferred to and agreed with him.

"You know, I have some cards in my desk if you want to write me a letter," he said, making it almost like a question but sounding manipulative enough for it to be a demand.

I said OK, and he led me to his desk. He told me to talk about how much I loved him and how much I wanted to be with him. As he pontificated, I wrote. I wish I could say I felt it because then it would have at least been a semi enjoyable experience, but I didn't. I didn't feel a thing he said I felt, so I just wrote. When I was done, I handed it to him. With the first few letters he had me write to him, I handed them over and never saw them again. It wasn't until a few months later that I opened up his desk drawer to find a stack of those letters stamped by the USPS—meaning he had mailed them—to himself!

Thankfully I was still friends with my little friend group from high school. To this day we're all still friends, no matter how much things change. They were my rocks. We were always together and getting into shenanigans. By the time I got to college, I was finally allowed to go to friends' houses, but not frequently, and I was never allowed to sleep over. They'd come over to my house, though, and swim in our pool and sleep over. Those moments were the ones that saved me. They're the ones that told me that life was going to be OK, no matter how messed up it got.

Jumping back to my high school years, Adder always found a way to but himself into every aspect of my life, including my friend group. One night, after he watched all of us swim at my parents' house, he approached me and said, "That Natalie, she really is beautiful, isn't she?"

"Uh, yeah," I said, shocked. "She is."

It was almost as if he was trying to make me jealous, trying to get a reaction out of me. The compliments kept flowing, but I just stared at him and agreed, playing it as neutral as possible.

It wasn't so much that I saw through his weird games, but rather that I truly was indifferent. The phrase "I don't care" is thrown around a lot these days. It's probably been thrown around for as long as men have had the ability to pester women. But when it came to Adder, when it came to my family, when it came to being a Syrian woman growing up and living in America, I had truly lost all will to care.

Like the many, many women who came before me, I was given a predetermined life. I was to go to school, get good grades, graduate, be introduced to a man who planned to marry me, have his children, and tend to his house for the rest of my life until the Lord welcomed me into the next life. It makes me think of Grandma and how she didn't really have any personal enjoyment, only obligations. Every time I think of her, I get sad because she truly lived a life of destitution. She never drove. She never worked a real job. She didn't have friends outside of the house. For as long as I knew her, she lived with us and helped my parents raise us kids. She cooked and cleaned, enjoyed family time, and nothing else. There was nothing for her. There was no passion. She went on for one hundred years existing—just existing, no more, no less. There was no trying to better herself, no trying to grow. She was just there, living that classic Syrian "When we die, we die" type of life. It was really sad. And I knew that I never ever wanted to live like that. I knew that if I ever had kids, I would make sure they never lived like that either. But how could I do that when I found myself living the same life as Grandma?

So to survive, I adopted the attitude of "I don't give a fuck." When Adder said things to get a reaction out of me, I ignored it. Maybe it was for survival, or maybe it was in my blood. Either way, it was the only way I knew how to deal with this sorry life I was living.

Eventually my friends started to notice how creepy it was that Adder was hanging out with us.

"You know, it's a little weird, like, how he is always around," Violet said to me one day. "He always tries to be funny, but he really isn't. Don't you think?"

"Yeah," I said, repeating the words "I don't care" to myself in order to avoid blowing my cover.

"No, I mean, like…every time we're in the pool, he's there. Don't you think that's weird?"

"Yeah," I said. "It's just the way he is, you know? He's always been that way. You just got to learn how to ignore him."

It ate me alive inside that I couldn't be honest with them. I couldn't even tell my best friends that I was in a relationship—granted, a relationship that I didn't want to be in, but a relationship nonetheless. Anytime that feeling of dishonesty got too intense, I masked it with "I don't care."

And the secrets built and built. They say that lying causes a snowball effect. You tell one lie, and it just gets bigger and bigger. Or maybe it's akin to a wall of spiderwebs. You weave one web and then another, thinking it'll be no big deal, but eventually, all of your webs grow so large that they start to impede on each other and eventually, you're covered in webs and can't move. Thus, I isolated myself from as many people as I could. The less I talked, the less I had to lie. And the less often there were people around, the more I could be myself, whoever that was. The more I could be alone in my web.

———— ◆ ————

It was hard going to school and seeing cute guys. I was young and excited to start living that classic American life, even though I knew I was still tethered to my parents and Adder. That dream of waking up in my life, but without all the strings attached, persisted. College was the time to be free, to talk to guys I found attractive, to go to house parties, to make new friends. I was ready to escape, but when I'd come back down to reality, I wasn't so ready.

One day Adder called me and told me we were breaking up.

"What?" I said.

"We're breaking up, Maia. It's over."

I was speechless. I didn't know what to say or how to react. I should have been happy, so why did I feel as if the whole world had just ended? Was it because I was being rejected by the lowest scum of the earth?

He told me it was because we just weren't ready for each other, that I was still so young. Young? You *just* realized, I thought. He told me that I deserved better and made me feel as if he were doing it for me. And he reminded me that I could never have another relationship per Syrian culture. In his words, I was "damaged goods." My heart broke.

"You've already had sex," he said. "That was a decision you made, and now you have to live with those consequences."

A decision I made? I thought. How did I make that decision?

Like any extreme form of gaslighting does to someone, I was crushed. I was only eighteen, yet there I was—damaged goods. A part of me was relieved; a huge weight had been lifted off my shoulders. No more lies, no more interactions with this predator. The other part was tied down with fear. How could I tell my parents I couldn't get married? How could I explain to them why I couldn't get married?

About six months after we "broke up," I got a call from Adder. He asked me if I was seeing anyone, and I said no. He said he wasn't surprised. The conversation was brief, but it was clear that he was trying to get back into my life.

I was still distraught by the breakup, trying to understand my place as a Syrian woman in this American world. It was confusing, and I felt broken. How could this have happened?

He called me again a few days later. He told me that he had been thinking about how I had yet to meet someone and how that made him sad. He told me that he still loved me and that he'd be willing to get back together with me because he just couldn't bear to think of me never being loved and that if I would have him, he'd love to get back together with me. So I said yes. I figured that was the only way to keep him from telling my parents about what happened.

One day, while we were at his apartment and he was feeling romantic, he sat down on the couch next to me and said, "You know, do you remember all those times I'd come over to the house when you were a kid?"

Of course I did.

"I noticed you," he said. "I've always loved you, Maia."

I shifted slightly, annoyed with where this was going but overwhelmed with a sense of *I don't care.*

"I remember one time, you bent over to pick something up," he said, putting his hand on my leg, "and I could see those beautiful breasts of yours. That was the first time I ever saw your breasts."

In that moment, at sixteen, I should have felt that he was always watching.

———————

"We have to show your parents that you're unhappy," Adder said to me out of nowhere.

"What do you mean?"

"We have to show them that you're so unhappy that you'd leave them."

I thought for a few moments—about the severity of this, what it would even look like, and more importantly, why— but of course, the only thing that came out of my mouth was "OK." At the time, I was confused. Why would I want to leave my family? Where would I even go? I loved my brothers dearly. Leaving them would traumatize me. In retrospect, it was to prepare for marriage.

He told me the plan. I was to write a letter to my parents explaining that they treated me like a child, that they didn't respect me or my choices, and I couldn't live like that anymore. I would place it on the table where they would see it. They still have that letter to this day. Then I was to pack up all of my belongings—yes, all of them—and during the day while my parents were working, stuff them into my car. I was to drive to his brother's house and tell his brother that I got into a fight with my parents.

"Why don't you tell him?" I asked.

"Because he's my brother, it would be weird coming from me"

Made sense, I guess.

I was to run away from home and never go back.

So I did. I packed up all of my belongings, and I left. When I got to his brother's house, I told him the story that had been fed to me, and he took me in.

For the most part, while I was at Adder's brother's house, Adder was at my parents' house, most likely consoling my parents. They had no idea where I was. They kept calling my cell phone, but I was instructed to ignore it, so I turned it off.

At some point while I was gone, Adder managed to get away from my parents to give his brother a ring on the phone and asked to speak with me Although we touched on the crisis at hand—me running away—we mostly just talked about life and love. He talked about our relationship, and how he was lucky that I was *willing* to defect from Syrian culture just to be with him. He made it seem like my choice.

"You know, we should get married one day."

I nearly choked.

"What?" I asked.

"We should get married one day. I mean, not now, obviously, but some day."

There was a long pause.

"OK," I said. *I don't care.*

"If we did it now, everyone would know something was up. Your parents would try to keep us apart. But if we did it when you were, oh, I don't know, say, maybe twenty, then they'd have no grounds to protest."

"OK," I said. *I don't care.*

The conversation ventured to other places, but my mind didn't. Was he serious? I was only eighteen. How could he be talking about marriage when I was just barely in college?

And while Adder was consoling my parents, he was taking note of their plans, if any. Eventually my parents decided to call the cops, and when the cops came saying that they were going to try to track my car and put out an APB, Adder called me at his brother's house and told me to pack up and go back home.

I was so scared to go home. What would my parents say? More importantly, what would I say? I hadn't wanted to leave home in the first place, and now I was going to have to lie about why I had done it?

My parents, of course, hugged me when I got home. And they cried. They made me promise that I would never leave again, and although I had no intentions of ever leaving them again, it was already sewn into my future.

CHAPTER 3

I Now Pronounce You

*Pretending you're okay is easier than having
to explain to everyone why you are not*
—Unknown

"Remember when I said we should get married a couple years ago?" Adder asked.

I didn't reply.

"Well, we've been together for a while. I think it's time."

It was the spring, and I was almost two years into college. I didn't know what would become of my life after school, but I was nearly to the point where I'd lost all hope. My younger self would have hoped and begged God that I would be freed from Adder's shackles, that I would be free from my parents, and that I could go off and start my own family. All I wanted was to be free. But that's a lot to ask for as a Syrian woman. And for Syrian women, being in charge of your own destiny is something precious you lose over time. By the time Adder brought up marriage again, I was on autopilot, saying yes whenever he made me think he wanted me to say yes.

On my twentieth birthday, he set the date for August 3rd. After we set the date, he said he would, as is traditional in Syria, ask for my hand in marriage. He said that he would reveal our relationship and inferred that my parents would eventually know everything about the two of us.

That's insane, I thought. They can't know that you preyed upon me when I was underage. They'd kill us! So of course, I told him that wasn't a good idea. In retrospect, I don't think he ever actually intended to tell my parents. He knew I would be too weak to confront them. Then he could act like he didn't tell them—for my sake—and take the credit. But adhering to *my* wishes, he didn't tell my parents.

He told me that we'd keep the marriage a simple church wedding. We found a priest in San Clemente, and Adder invited a few of his family members. He told me that none of my family could come, that they couldn't find out until after, otherwise they'd go insane.

"I have to have someone there for me," I said. "I have to."

There was a pause in our conversation as he just stared at me, totally unimpressed.

"What about Violet and Jessica?" he asked, referring to my two best friends.

"OK. But they don't know anything about us," I said. "What, am I just going to say, 'Oh yeah, by the way, I'm getting married to my dad's best friend. You should come'?"

"Listen, we both know that you all are adults, and adults don't share every aspect of their lives, even with best friends," he said. "Just tell them that we've been seeing each other for a few years. I think you should tell them that we started seeing each other when you were eighteen."

Because the truth—sixteen—was unspeakable. So there I was, once again, playing the parrot.

To some, the parrot symbolizes the virginal Mother Mary. In many cultures, this majestic creature is regarded as a miracle because of its ability to imitate and reproduce human speech. Many nights that summer, I lay awake thinking about how beautiful the parrot was, yet I was so far from majestic and even further from a miracle.

When I finally told Violet, she was shocked.

"Is this really what you want?" she asked. She was the first person I had told about our relationship since it had begun more than four years before. Her concern for me evoked a deep sorrow within me. I wanted to cry. But instead, I played the role that he had asked me to play. I told her that we loved each other and that this was forever. Every word that came out of my mouth was complete and utter bullshit.

"Then I guess I'll support you," she said. I wanted so desperately to tell her the truth. I tried so hard that I thought the truth was seeping out of my eyes. Maybe, just maybe, she can see the truth in my eyes if I force it hard enough, I thought. But she didn't. And if she did, she didn't say anything. She agreed to be my maid of honor.

When I was a little girl, I dreamed often about getting married. I always knew I wanted to be a mother and a wife, to be my own person, to be more than what my culture typically allowed. I saw what was possible in America. And I wanted it. I dreamed of browsing the aisles of the dress shop trying to find that perfect dress, that dress that made my jaw drop and brought a tear to my mom's eyes. Violet and I went dress shopping after I told her, and although it was exciting, I knew it was wrong. I knew that it was a mistake, and that nugget of information sat in the back of my mind, preventing me from being truly in the moment. When I finally found a dress I could settle on, I tried it on. When I looked in the mirror, instead of seeing an angel, I saw a prison. That dress symbolized being trapped forever. My life was over.

Despite being on autopilot, on the rare occasion, I had the wherewithal to ponder escape. I thought about leaving him. I thought about running away. But every time I got serious about setting my life straight, the reminder of our Syrian culture set right back in. He reminded me—unknowingly, at the right times—that I could never tell my parents what happened. And if I ever left him, he would most certainly tell them, although he only ever inferred that. And if my parents ever did find out, I'd be sorry. It got to the point where I just wanted to get married because that, in my mind, would solve everything. My parents wouldn't have to know about the non-consensual sex. In a way, I was saving my parents from social suicide, Adder suggested to me, almost in a tactical fashion. I made the choice to marry him in order to protect my family from any shame and to protect the family name. How ironic, the truth finally coming out after fighting so hard to keep it hidden.

On the day of the wedding, Adder's relative walked me down the aisle in my gorgeous wedding dress. All of it was nice—the church, the dress, my friends—except for the most important parts: my groom and the absence of my family.

I don't remember much about the wedding other than the daze I was in. I felt numb. Leading up to the event, I expected to feel angry. I was enraged by the fact that I felt like this man was holding me hostage, in a sense, even though he legally wasn't. And I thought I'd be angry with myself for not doing more, for not pushing harder to get out. But I didn't. All I felt was numb. I played the part I was expected to play—a gorgeous bride, smiling and walking down the aisle. There was nothing I could do, so I went with it. I stood next to him, our hands held tightly. I listened as much as I could, trying to keep my thoughts from wandering. I looked him in the eyes and forced a smile every time the priest said something sweet. I smiled when Adder said, "I do." And I smiled when I said, "I do." I tried not to think of my parents and family. I tried not to think about the aftermath. And when I realized it was time to kiss, I leaned in and conjured up enough passion to make it seem real.

After we were wed, we walked back down the aisle, headed through the doors and into the limo. Our luggage in tow, we were off to the airport for our honeymoon in Florida. I changed dresses and kept my tiara on and hair in place.

Unbeknownst to me, before the wedding, Adder had spoken with our priest and asked him to call my dad and ask him to come to the church once we boarded the plane for Miami. At that point, he would inform my father of my nuptials while I was off to celebrate. As we waited in line to board the plane, Adder asked me to turn my phone off and to keep it off until he said so. He said we would deal with my parents when we got back and that he didn't want anything to ruin our celebration.

We sat next to each other, but not like how I thought married couples sat. I had always had this vision that married couples snuggled up on planes, that they held hands and the wife leaned her head on his shoulder. We did none of these things. We just sat there. He was as thrilled as he could be; I was still in a haze.

The flight attendant walked by, looked at Adder, looked at me, leaned in, and asked him, "Did your daughter just win a beauty pageant?"

"This is my wife," he said. "We're on our honeymoon."

The sweet flight attendant, who I'm sure felt some sense of embarrassment—despite her intuition being close to right—apologized and moved us up to first class. He took me by the hand, and we walked up to first class. Thinking back to those moments, I never felt like his wife. I felt like his object, his obsession. And if he had asked me how I felt, maybe I would have told him, but he never did. Who was I kidding? I wasn't powerful enough to actually say that to him.

———◆———

On our first day, we traveled down to the Keys and Adder's entire back got sunburned—to the point of blisters. The misery set in, but we tried to enjoy it the best we could—beach time, restaurants, everything touristy we could find.

"You know you won't be able to talk to your family for a while, right?" Adder asked me during our first dinner. Something about his demeanor had changed since we kissed at the altar. He was happy—happier than I'd ever seen him, actually—but he seemed to be more commanding, more authoritative, and not in the best way. In essence, and for lack of better words, he had an aura of control.

"Why?"

"Because they'll be too angry. Just give me some time, and I'll figure out how, but until then, you cannot communicate with them."

I was shocked and confused, but as the wife, I knew I wasn't allowed to question it.

I had always assumed that once you got married, you stopped paying attention to or noticing attractive people around you. But then again, my marriage wasn't normal, so how could I expect to operate under normal assumptions? I enjoyed the trip, for the most part because I kept my mind from thinking about what I did. I noticed all these cute couples on vacation. They just fit, they looked like they belonged together and were having so much fun. In a way it was tough because there I was with this older man. I was embarrassed at people seeing me with him because we always got *the look*. You know, the look that suggested that I was a gold digger, and he was the mine. I wondered if they looked at me and thought, she's so pretty, why is she with that old guy? I wondered if they assumed he had money and that was why I was there.

We stayed in Florida for ten days, exploring the Keys and Miami, and traveling up to Jacksonville to visit his family for a couple of days. It was a little awkward, given that they had a small house full of kids. Being around his family made me yearn for mine. I still felt trapped in my wedding dress and wanted nothing more than to curl up on the couch next to my parents and brothers.

When we got back home, we were greeted by a massive number of messages from my parents, asking what was going on and if I was OK. I had never heard their voices so panicked, so upset, so confused.

I told Adder about the flurry of messages and how I thought I should call them.

"I don't think you should," he said.

"Why?"

"Well, I called them, and——" he paused. "I don't know how to tell you this, Maia. They are really angry with me. I just don't think you should talk to them. We're married now, so if they don't want to talk to me, then why should you talk to them?"

"Wait, you called them? When you told me that I couldn't even talk to them?"

I'd never seen a look of sedentary rage before—I didn't even think it was possible—but there it was, plastered on his face. I knew he was mad, but by God, it was so cleverly disguised.

"Do you trust me or not?" he asked. "Because if not, we can just go ahead and get a divorce. Is that what you want?"

You've lost your mind, I thought, but instead said, "Of course not. I was just confused."

"You're damn right you were confused. They don't want to talk to me, and we're married now, so you're going to trust me on this. We're one. If they're going to talk to you, they need to accept me as well. By the way, I also talked to the priest. He called your dad to tell him we eloped. He said your dad just dropped to the ground and started crying."

Why was he telling me this? Just hearing that felt like a knife in my heart. I couldn't believe I had made my dad cry. I was so heartbroken with how much pain I caused my family.

The only thing I kept reminding myself was that I did it for them. The other option would have been ten times worse for them.

Later that night, while washing dishes, I thought maybe I'd been too harsh on him, that maybe I wasn't trusting him enough. Maybe he was so upset because of how fresh everything was; maybe it truly hurt him that his best friend was upset with him. Give it time, I thought. It's not like you can go on never seeing your family again. That would be absurd.

And then it hit me—the weight of my entire life came crashing in as a harsh reminder that I hadn't been able to talk to my parents for months. I had been living a lie. I had been living so unhappily. A plate slipped from my hands and crashed into the sink. I clutched onto the counter to hold myself up as my body gave way. Adder came rushing in, asked why I was crying, then put his arm around me. I told him that I just wanted to talk to my dad; what I would have given to talk to my dad. It was that kind of uncontrollable crying, with snot running down the person holding you where even if you want to stop crying, you just can't. It lasted for what felt like thirty years, until finally he told me I could call my dad—but only my dad. When I composed myself, he said that he had to be present for the call so he could hear what was going on.

Sure, I was nervous about disappointing my dad. I was scared of what he would say about me, about my marriage. But I still wanted to talk to him. I needed to talk to him. My mom, on the other hand, I was petrified to speak with. Would she hate me? Would she disown me? I didn't want to lose my parents.

The goal of the call, Adder said, was to fix his relationship with my father. They were dear friends; my dad was upset with

Adder because I married him, so it was my responsibility to fix this. And I believed that. We practiced what I was going to say for about an hour. Eventually, over time, we'd work up to going over to their house again, but at that point, we were to speak only over the phone. Adder just wanted to be accepted again, he claimed, and I believed that.

I drank a glass of water, then picked up the receiver and dialed. The sound of my dad's voice was so foreign. It even sounded different from the man who had left me all those voicemails. It felt raw, brutalized.

"It's me," I said.

There was a long pause with hushed breathing from the other end.

No answer. "I'm sorry."

I could hear the pain through the phone without him having to say a word., This sent me into another frenzy. I cried, and I apologized to him. I did most of the talking—explaining—just trying to cling to all the time I could, trying to cling to whatever was left of our relationship. The call only lasted about ten minutes. I looked over to my left to see Adder tapping his watch as if to tell me we had been talking for too long and that I needed to hang up.

I told my dad that I'd call him again the next week.

———— •• ————

From the moment we got off the plane from Florida, I felt like I was stuck in a perpetual state of nothingness. I didn't experience much emotion other than sadness. It may have been a form of depression; I'm not sure. All I'm sure of is that I was a blob. When your every move is directed by another human, when you are essentially a puppet, it translates into your emotions, and you become nothing other than a shell of yourself. You become a ghost. You simply live to survive. I can't imagine I was fun to live with—ghosts never are—but then again, I'm not sure if he even cared. Part of me wishes I had some sort of insight into his thinking, but the other part of me is so damn grateful that I didn't. I wonder often if he truly loved me, and I think in some weird, narcissistic way, he did. But I don't think it was ever true love.

I was allowed to call my father every week for fifteen minutes—no more—for the first few months of our marriage. After about two or three months, it stopped.

"You know," Adder said after about two or three months when I went for the phone, "if they loved you, they'd reach out to you once in a while. They wouldn't wait for your call."

"What do you mean?" I asked.

"When's the last time they called you? Hmm?"

I said nothing.

"Exactly. They don't love you, Maia," he said. "I think you shouldn't call them anymore. If they love you, you'll hear from them."

And just like that, I believed him. The phone calls stopped.

In August of 2001, right before our one-year anniversary, Adder's mother and sister came to stay with us from Syria. It was interesting being around his family for this long and seeing what morals and values they held and how those correlated to Adder.

I didn't mind their company in the house, but the day before they were supposed to leave, I felt an odd sense of relief. The next day, I walked out into the kitchen and found his mother packing up her belongings, but his sister was not doing the same.

I pulled Adder aside. "Your sister isn't packing her things. Is she OK? She has to fly out today."

"Oh," he said with a look of confidence, "she's going to be staying with us."

I was crushed. Not so much because she was staying with us but because I wasn't consulted about the decision. Here we were in a marriage that was portrayed as a partnership but in reality was a dictatorship. And this decision was the final nail in the coffin, as it solidified his power position. What I wanted, it seemed, came second to what he wanted. It was a general lack of respect.

The next week was our one-year anniversary, which I was looking forward to. I always looked forward to special moments like holidays and anniversaries because they were special moments in which everything felt normal. Every other day of our life together felt like a massive pit of confusion and irreverence. It felt not normal. But on special days like holidays and anniversaries, we were able to forget about this crazy lifestyle that we lived—that he didn't even realize we were living. I could forget about all of the animosity I held deep inside and pretend like we had a normal little family.

I woke up on our anniversary excited. I had never had an anniversary before, so I wasn't sure what to expect. And although I wasn't sure what to expect, there were things that I certainly did not expect. The day was steeped in excitement, so when Adder told me that we were going somewhere, I eagerly embarked. I put some light curls in my hair and did my face up all pretty. We got in the car and drove down the street, and when he pulled into the parking lot of an immigration lawyer's office, I figured it was part of some elaborate plan. Could a man really be treating me to such an exciting surprise? I was thrilled. When we got out and walked up to the door, the excitement started to fade and I asked, "What are we doing here?"

"We're submitting my application for a green card," he said so matter-of-factly. "It's been a year now, and unless you want me to get deported, you have to help me fill out the paperwork."

I was in disbelief! How could he spend our anniversary doing this?

And that's exactly how we spent it. We sat there for hours filling out paperwork.

At the time I didn't know anything. I was so naive. It was just another example of how everything he did was calculated. He used me just to get his citizenship and then used that to bring his entire family over.

———•———

One day a few months later, I realized that my period was late. We had never really talked about having a baby. Up until that point, my life had been on autopilot, so I guess it shouldn't have come as a shock when I found out I was pregnant. Everything was going according to his plan, despite us never having a conversation about anything. We had been married for a year, which meant it was baby time. It was mechanical, you know?

I still remember that moment of being flooded with joy and desire. Until that point, I had never wanted something more. If it's a girl, I thought, I hope she doesn't have my hair or my nose.

When I hear other mothers talk about the first time they found out they were pregnant, they seem to always talk about how they realized their important role, realized that they would have to grow up. Of course I experienced that too, but more than anything, I knew that I wanted her to grow up completely differently than how I grew up. I don't want to be strict, I thought. There would be boundaries and rules, sure, but I wanted her to go out with her friends. I wanted her to do activities that she wanted to do. I wanted her to be a kid. I wanted her to feel like she could talk to me about anything, to feel safe with me—to trust me. I wanted an open-dialogue relationship with her. I wanted her so badly.

In the mornings, I always craved salad with a lot of lemon. Eventually that craving morphed into spaghetti, and there was no question as to whether or not I would get it. And I'll give it to him—Adder was attentive and caring. If I demanded Lucky Charms, oh, I got Lucky Charms. And when I had morning sickness for five months, he helped me to the bathroom. I was still finishing up my degree, so when I'd drive to class, I'd set a plastic bag in my lap so I could hurl on the freeway if I didn't have time to pull over.

When I was eight months pregnant, I walked across the stage at my graduation to get that degree I had worked so hard for. Pride doesn't describe the feeling I experienced in that moment. With a baby on the way and a husband who seemed to want to keep me away from the world, I wondered what use a piece of paper would be anyway. But I tried not to think about it, instead focusing on the fact that I was one of the first women in my family to achieve this much success.

─────◆─────

A few months before I gave birth, my father was in a terrible accident. While driving down the street, he lost consciousness for a few seconds after a brief bout of dizziness and hit another car. He was taken to the hospital. One evening Adder sat me down and told me about what had happened, casually leaving out the part about how he found out, and I didn't have the nerve to ask.

"It's serious," Adder said.

"Then we need to go see him," I said, concerned about the severity.

"Well, that's the thing," he said, "I didn't want to tell you this way, but honey, I'm sorry. He doesn't want to see you."

"Well, how do you know?"

"He specifically said he didn't want to see you. You broke his heart."

I broke his heart? Me? In retrospect, it was silly of me to believe that my dad didn't want to see me, but I knew I did break his heart when I married Adder so it seemed possible.

As my due date got closer, I heard less and less about my father's condition; I only knew that he was still not doing well. My dad was my kryptonite. The fact that he didn't want to see his only daughter broke my heart, and I sobbed relentlessly.

─────◆─────

On July 1, 2002, my precious Jaeda was born. I thought I was going to die. It was the most excruciating pain of my life. They were supposed to give me an epidural, but when I arrived, the anesthesiologist was in another surgery, so they told me I would have to go without. You've got to be kidding me, I thought. The pain was unbearable, and the only way my body knew how to combat it was to fight. I screamed at probably every nurse and doctor I could find, but the battle was a losing one.

I asked the doctor to check me because I was convinced that I was ready to give birth—finally. The pain somehow kept getting worse, and I was ready to get this over with. They always say that you'll want to remember moments like those forever—and don't get me wrong, I will—but I was ready for it to be a memory.

"You're only at three centimeters," the doctor said.

"What?" I asked. "Check again. You've got it wrong."

The doctor laughed and walked to the other side of the room, most likely because he knew I was ready to throw something—with love, of course.

The pain continued, yet a deeper pain flamed inside of me. I was mad as hell that my parents weren't there and even madder that I was the one who had rejected them. I wanted so badly for them to be there to witness this magical moment, yet how could I let them when my father, according to Adder, had rejected me? If I wasn't welcome in his hospital room, why should he be in mine? You see, that's the scary part of it all—I was led to believe Adder's web of lies. The manipulation he used was amplified drastically, and my fear was becoming uncontrollable.

Finally, after what felt like three hundred years, they gave me an epidural and I became myself again. I don't know who

I was before, but I didn't know her and I didn't care to. And the moment I saw my baby's face, I forgot it all. Suddenly, it all became worth it. At 1:10 p.m. on July 1, my little angel was born at seven pounds, ten ounces, and twenty-and-a-half inches.

When I saw her face for the first time, I cried, the same kind of snotty cry that I had on the phone with my parents. How could I have become so lucky? What had I done to deserve this little cherub? I held her so close, promising to always protect her, to love her for eternity and beyond, to be her mother the best way I knew how. Adder put one hand on me and another on our precious baby, and we both cried. Despite everything we had gone through, despite everything he had put me through, there was love in that room that day. There was love in my tears, and there was love in his tears. Our souls sat still and quiet, and everything we had been through was forgotten. It was a moment of humanity, a moment of human touch. My love for my daughter was so strong, and I wanted nothing more than to make the world perfect for her. Whatever transgressions had occurred between me and Adder, I wanted to be forgiven. I wanted everything to be OK. I wanted love.

———◆———

Holding my sweet Jaeda was surreal. Even though I had nine months to prepare for the feeling of holding my baby, nothing could have prepared me for what I experienced. And before her birth, although we were married, I never really got a sense of family. The only feeling of family that I had ever known had been with my parents and brothers. That was family. With

Adder, it certainly felt like more than friends, but saying that it felt like family just didn't sit right with me. There was something off. But after Jaeda was born, when we would sit in the living room or go for walks, suddenly it felt different. Our little family was three. I never wanted to be a typical Syrian wife, but I sure was willing to do what I had to in order to make our family succeed.

That feeling, as strong as it may have been, wasn't strong enough. The more I got to know my beautiful daughter, the more I learned about the world.

One gorgeous Los Angeles morning, I took Jaeda to the park. We watched the children play and the dogs run. We mingled with a few other mothers and their children. Life was good, aside from the lingering feeling of uneasiness. It was a little nugget in the pit of my stomach, and I couldn't quite figure out what it meant or why it was there.

Our little family of three was perfect, so why did I get the feeling that all was not OK? Should this have been a surprise given that I had been chased by this feeling of impending doom my entire life? To combat the feeling, I did the only thing I could—I picked up Jaeda and held her. After a few minutes of snuggling on the park bench, I held her face up to mine and looked into her eyes. She was precious. She had an entire life ahead of her, yet her eyes seemed to hold all of the secrets of the world. This child, who couldn't even talk, somehow seemed to know more than me. She smiled at me so innocently, and I started to cry.

What the fuck have I done, I thought as I sobbed. Jaeda's smile broke, and she looked confused. I snuggled her in my arms and cried some more.

What did I do to my parents? I thought. How could I have abandoned them like this? What am I going to do when Jaeda gets older? What if the same thing happens to her? I took all of these beautiful moments away from my parents. How did that make them feel?

In that moment, I realized my responsibility. I realized the weight of my behavior. I realized my complicity. I realized that my parents must have been heartbroken, and I felt like shit. I held Jaeda closer and asked her to learn from my mistakes. I asked her to forgive me. I said a silent prayer and asked God to ask my parents for forgiveness. I just wanted them to forgive me.

I did everything I could to ignore those thoughts, given that there wasn't really anything I could do. I wasn't allowed to speak with my parents unless Adder was there, which meant I had no way of saying I was sorry again. So I thought about other things. I consumed myself with being a mother full-time. Growing up, I wished and hoped that I would get to take on whatever career I wanted. I had a feeling I wouldn't be able to, but I still hoped. Yet somewhere along the line, I forgot about all of that. I forgot about what my future could have been, what I had always dreamed of my future being. And no matter how much I wanted to be a mother, I didn't imagine that I would become a full-time, stay-at-home mom. But that's exactly what Adder wanted me to be.

That doesn't mean that I would have given that time up, in retrospect. I'm grateful for every second I got to spend with Jaeda.

When she started nursing, it was the best feeling ever, despite it being physically an excruciating experience. For the first few days, she didn't eat, and it seemed as if I called the doctor every five seconds. I realized that I had been calling far too much when finally, after what was probably my twentieth call, they told me that I needed to calm down. I was shocked, but it was what I needed to hear.

"She's not going to die on the first day of not eating," the nurse told me. That seemed to be quite a harsh response despite the number of times I called. It's incredible how the sense of responsibility, the need to do whatever you have to in order to protect your children, can make you forget about common sense.

———

The worst part about me being a stay-at-home mom was that I rarely got alone time with Jaeda because Keres, Adder's sister, and their mother, Claudia, were always in the house and they always wanted to be around Jaeda, to hold her to get to experience that new-baby experience, and I don't blame them. There is something ethereal and jovial about being with a new baby, and I had to keep reminding myself that it was Claudia's first grandchild and Keres's first niece. Jealousy reared its head quite frequently, but at the time, I didn't realize that it was just that—jealousy. It seemed as if they were trying to take possession of my baby—always holding her, even when she napped. There was even a moment where I had to bite my tongue so as not to say, "You know, you can't hold her all day, even when she sleeps." And I'm grateful that I didn't because now I realize it was just that—jealousy, caused by me just wanting to be as close to my daughter as I possibly could at every moment of the day, even when I was tired.

No matter how caught up in my own mind I got, it still felt it was valid for me to wonder why Adder had asked them to move in in the first place. Was it because he didn't trust me?

Was it because he wanted someone to constantly be around to watch out for the baby, to make sure that I wasn't sneaking around or going to see my parents? It felt like more of a security measure than him just wanting to be with his family. It was exhausting.

Thankfully I thought of them as family, at least in the beginning. And maybe that's just because I was so hopeful that things were still going to be normal. I truly believed that all of the oddities occurring in my life—being coaxed into a marriage, his family living with us, me living without my family—were just temporary. It would take about a year before I realized that this could be forever. All I wanted was my space, my freedom. That little sliver of hope that I had always had as a child that I would experience true freedom. All I wanted was time with my kid alone, yet I was made to feel like I was asking for too much.

On a humid Los Angeles afternoon in August of 2002, the three of us—Jaeda, Keres, and I—went to the grocery store. When we pulled into the parking lot, I spotted my mom parking a few spots down from us. Despite the fact that she lived in the area and it was not out of the ordinary for my mom to go grocery shopping, I was still overcome with panic, thinking, Oh my God, what is she doing here? I knew that I was going to get in trouble, even though it was random. I thought somehow he was going to be pissed. Keres told me to calm down and just get out of the car like normal.

As if I lived in a movie, my mom spotted us and started to approach, causing me to freeze. I thought that anything I could possibly do would be wrong and the blame would be cast on me. I kept Jaeda in the car, and Keres used her body to block the door. I can't remember all of what was said, only that it was more of a shout than an average-toned speaking.

"Is that my granddaughter?" I remember hearing my mom ask.

Fear stilled me, and I said nothing.

"Is that my granddaughter?" she said, a bit louder, trying to push past Keres. "I'm going to see my granddaughter!"

I was still frozen.

Almost in an instant, Keres shoved my mom, pushing her to the ground, and yet I still stood there frozen. My mom—the woman who birthed and raised me, the woman who only ever cared for me—was attacked. I just stood there. What kind of asshole doesn't help her own mom? I asked myself. The shame that set in was pungent, it was hurtful, it was deep.

But apparently my mom didn't need my help because she leaped from the ground and yanked Keres by the hair, throwing her off to the side of the car and successfully shoving herself into the car to see Jaeda. She lifted the screen that was covering Jaeda's car seat, still shoving Keres off from her. For the first time, my beautiful mom was able to look her granddaughter in the eyes. Despite the chaos and madness, Jaeda remained blissful, and I sat there cold and frozen. And just like that, my mom walked away, a smile on her face. The smile had nothing to do with succeeding in the brawl; I could tell that it was the pure joy of seeing her granddaughter—her flesh and blood—in the flesh.

Keres called Adder, who was at work, and told him what had happened. He demanded that we return home, and Keres submitted to the order. I cried the entire way back.

It's hard to explain the dichotomy that was occurring in my mind at the time. Looking back, I see that deep down I knew what side was the right side to be on. I knew that what Adder had done to me was wrong. I knew that not talking to my parents was wrong—hence my sobbing the entire way home—but at the time, on the surface level, I was upset with my mom. In my mind, I would do anything for my kids— rational or not—so at the time, I didn't understand why my mom wouldn't act that way too. I think that misplaced sense of resentment really came into play when I thought about all of the things I would do for my daughter. No matter what the situation, I would never let anything come between me and my daughter, and I would do anything to see her and be a part of her life, so why couldn't my own mom do that for me?

It was later that I realized it was most likely just a difference in how we were raised and the cultures from which we came. I the Americanized Syrian, she the traditional Syrian, where pride and respect is never compromised

---

In early 2003 I found out I was pregnant again. Just as before, there was no planning, there was no conversation; it just happened, and I couldn't have been more thrilled. All my life I had wanted to be a mother, and here I was going to have a second child. I had always wanted my kids to be close in age because I wanted them to be friends.

Adder's temper had gotten worse, and although our marriage wasn't anywhere close to perfect (what a funny word "perfect" is, anyway), I still was happy about the new life we were shepherding into the world. At the ultrasound in February, we decided we would wait to learn the sex until the birth. Despite not knowing, I prayed that it would be a boy because I had always dreamed of having one boy and one girl. And so it was. And so God answered my prayers.

Aden was born on June 28, 2004, at 4:46 p.m., at seven pounds, eleven ounces, and twenty-one inches. We named Jaeda after a supermodel because we knew she would be even more beautiful than a supermodel. For Aden, we knew we wanted a more Americanized name but one with a deep meaning, so as to follow a tradition. Adder was thrilled that he had gotten a boy as it had always been his dream. He had the ideal image of being an American dad, tossing a ball to his son in the yard and teaching him how to drive and shave. So we named him after Adder's father.

But after Aden was born, things started to get worse. Mentality-wise, because of my Syrian upbringing, I was against divorce. I knew that I was stuck in this relationship with the father of my children and that I needed to make things right, to smooth things over. Not to mention the fact that even if I wasn't against divorce, I knew I could never leave because Adder's temper was too sporadic. How could I risk leaving my children with no mother? I loved them too much.

I tried convincing him to make his sister move out of the house, but he was against it. I even tried to pull the "it's her or me" card, which was met with a brutal verbal blow to my sanity, his calling me stupid and threatening me with divorce (and subsequently shame from the Syrian community). Eventually I wore him down, and he agreed that she would stay with us for "just a few more months." But of course, a few more months turned into just a few more, and then just one more year, and one more after that. It was never-ending. There I was, stuck with his family when I couldn't even talk to or see my own. It was like psychological torture, and it left me craving and yearning for my family. All I wanted was to hug my father and talk to my mom. I wanted to see my brothers, and I wanted to laugh with them again. All I wanted to do was laugh with them again.

His temper got worse, and his family got more annoying. They were his spies, and no matter what I did, I had to be careful, lest I do anything that may look suspicious, causing them to report back and causing him to lash out at me. I was a prisoner in my own home with my own children bearing witness. I loved my kids more than anything, and I found the mental capability to disconnect my feelings for them from my feelings toward Adder. Eventually, I grew to despise Adder, but I never let that come in between my feelings toward my children—the loves of my life. It's a talent of disassociation. Or is it simply just pure love? Is it simply the power of a mother's love?

I missed my family, and his temper made the feeling deeper. I wanted my children to know their grandparents, and after years of not speaking to them, it seemed as if they never would know them. That's when I decided I had had enough. I developed a plan to see my parents behind Adder's back. It was risky, I knew, for if he found out, I would be subjected to his furry.

CHAPTER 4

Stand By Your Man?

*A river cuts through rock, not because of
its power, but because of its persistence.*
—James Watkins

All I wanted was a normal life, and I was confused as to why I wasn't allowed to see my parents or other family members. It wouldn't have hurt Adder to let me see my family, to let our children see their grandparents. It wouldn't have hurt to have lived a normal life. That's all I have ever wanted—a normal life. To make matters worse, my parents only lived ten minutes away, so I just didn't understand.

When Aden was about three months old, I found out that my brother Drew, was having surgery on his stomach. I had reached my tipping point and desperately needed to see my family, to make amends.

"I'm going to visit Drew in the hospital," I said to Adder.

"No you're not," he said. "If you're going to go, don't bother coming back here. If you leave this house, don't even think about returning."

I marched into the kitchen and made sure that there was plenty of pumped milk in a bottle for Aden, then told Adder that I would be back in a couple of hours. I walked right out the door, and when I got to my car, I sighed with the greatest relief I think I have ever felt. I was shocked by my strength in confronting him face-to-face for the first time. I had always felt like a second mother to Drew, so there was no way I could not go to support him. I had to gain the courage.

As hard as it was to stand up to Adder and have the courage to go do what I felt I had to do and wanted to do for my family, it was just as hard not knowing what their reaction was going to be. I was nervous to confront them after all that time, but surprisingly, it was like they had just seen me yesterday. There was no questioning; there was no third-degree. I could see they were shocked, but they quickly hugged me and accepted me back into the family. They asked me how the kids were and how I was doing, just like everything was cool. I could tell they were happy that I had gotten the strength to be there, and I could tell they were proud.

Sick and tired of experiencing the deepest sorrow of my life, I decided it was time to finally see my parents again. I concocted a plan to take Aden, who obviously could not speak at the time, to see his grandparents while Adder was at work. It was by far the riskiest move I think I have ever made because if he were to call me while I was at my parents' and if I were to not answer, his suspicion would have been raised as at that point I had become the ultimate stay-at-home mother. It was my responsibility to be at his literal beck and call at every moment of every day.

The first time I went to visit, I thought I was having a heart attack because my heart raced so fast and a pain shot up my arm. It was a form of stress that I had not felt so intensely in years. But I must say that it was the greatest reward to see the look of joy in my parents' eyes as they played with their first and only grandson.

Honestly, the details didn't really register until later. It was an out-of-body experience, and my anxiety was at an all-time high. It was almost as if I blinked and then it was over.

—◆—

I'm not sure if he found out about my visits because he followed me or because he had someone else follow me. Maybe he had a tracker on me, or maybe a friend saw me at the gas station around the corner from my parents' house. Either way, Adder found out about my escapades after the fifth or sixth visit, and he confronted me about it not even one minute after he walked through the front door after work one day.

"Were you at your parents' house today?" he asked, but really demanded.

I paused. Should I lie? Should I run? I wasn't sure, so I played it safe.

"What do you mean?"

"You were at your parents' house today. Why were you at your parents' house today, Maia? Don't even think about fucking lying to me."

I'm not sure what overcame me or why a sense of fearlessness—albeit very, very small bits of fearlessness—enveloped me, but it did, and I rode the adrenaline high. Maybe it was the look on my daughter's face, the mirror that her look provided me.

"I wanted to see them," I said confidently. "What's wrong with wanting to see my parents? They wanted to see me, and I wanted to see them." I turned around and walked toward the kitchen.

"Don't walk away from me," he said, pushing past me to stand in front of me.

I straightened my posture and stood at a point where my breath and his could dance. I remembered that look in Jaeda's eyes, that innocence. I felt the fear of something similar happening to her. I couldn't imagine her growing up, going to college, and getting married, all without me in the picture. I took that away from my parents, and I felt the deepest regret. I felt like a piece of shit. If Jaeda ever did that to me, I thought, I would die.

"Imagine if someone did that to your daughter, Adder," I said. "Fucking imagine it!"

We were face-to-face; he paused, and his mouth closed.

"I want you to imagine it. What would you do if someone separated you from your daughter and told her she couldn't see you anymore?"

"I would kill him," he said, a twinkle of rage in his eyes.

"Exactly! But you want my parents to be understanding, Adder. You want them to forgive you and act as if you did nothing wrong, but if someone did that to your daughter, it would be unforgivable and you would kill him."

There was a pause as the anger plateaued in him.

"It's dif—"

"I'm not done," I said. "You can't even comprehend a middle ground or a compromise. You can't even stop to wonder if maybe, just maybe, you did something wrong. You can't even admit that maybe you did something wrong, Adder."

An anger-tinged "No" escaped through his teeth.

"And I don't feel bad for lying to you because you put me in that situation. This is your fault." I pushed past him, making my way to Jaeda's room.

"You are not allowed to ever—and I mean *ever*—do that again," he said as I walked away. "Do you understand me?"

Even though I had finally stood up for myself, I knew that I could never do it again. He was onto me, and I understood what he meant by "ever." Because, really, what *would* happen if I disobeyed him? The adrenaline wore off and was nearly immediately replaced by fear. I learned something about myself that night, but no matter how powerful that thing was, I was still back at square one, only this time, with more confidence.

In June of that year, Adder allowed Drew and my younger cousins to attend the kids' birthday party—they were turning two and four. It was the first time anyone from my side of the family had been welcome in our sphere, and I sobbed when I invited them. At the party I had the most fun I think I had had in years, simply because my family was there with me. Adder had allowed me this very minor thing, but it felt like the world. In retrospect, I'm made sad by the level of control he exhibited over me. I'm made sad by how little I had. I was deprived of so much, so when I got so little, I didn't take it for granted. And I still don't to this day.

"I want a divorce," I said to Adder not too long after that.

He said nothing.

"I want a normal life," I said after getting no response. "I'm not asking for too much or anything unreasonable."

He glanced at me again and said nothing, so we sat in silence. The courage it took me to work up to that was tough to muster.

"No," he finally said.

"No?"

"No. And if you do…"

We sat in silence some more, the tension percolating and my palms sweating.

"If you do, I will kill every single one of your family members. In front of you."

Then it was my turn to say nothing.

"And you think I won't?" he asked, getting up and moving over to the drawer where he kept his gun. He pulled it out, twisted it in his hands while he seemingly admired it. "And if you ever think about taking my children, I'll kill you next. So yes, I mean no."

The next day I called my father and told him what happened.

"Bring me the gun right now," he urged. "Get the gun and kids, and come here now."

My dad wanted me to leave everything, but I wasn't ready for that. I still had hope that our life could work out somehow. So I left the kids with Claudia but took the gun to my father's.

If I didn't get rid of that gun, I wouldn't be around much longer to even consider what I would do next. I told my father everything that Adder had said, and he told me that I wasn't going back to the house.

My father called our church's deacon to see if he could facilitate some common ground. We went to Royal Oaks Park in Duarte. As soon as Adder arrived, my father confronted him, which sparked a flurry of accusations and shouting. The chaos hurt so much. I just wanted everything to be calm, even if for just one moment. After a few moments of not being able to take it, I jumped in and yelled, asking them to stop fighting. The deacon wanted me to return home with Adder—to complete our home again—but my father refused to return the gun and certainly didn't want me to go home.

How could I abandon my children? I couldn't. That was never an option, and I knew I needed to go back at some point to get my kids. I didn't care if he was going to use the gun on me tomorrow, as long as I got my kids and they were safe.

The next day Adder went to the police station to report that my father had stolen his gun. The police station called my dad and told him he was to give it back. My dad insisted on dropping it off at the station so it would be documented.

———

Adder started letting me go to my parents' house once a month for three hours. At the time I was so shocked that I kept thinking to myself, Jesus! I can never find someone better than him! I had been so brainwashed and manipulated that it took quite some time to realize that I could, in fact, find someone better than him. But until then I was stuck in prison with Adder as my warden granting me little bits of exercise time in the yard.

Slowly that time went from three hours once a month to three hours every two weeks, and then right back to lockdown. And what was worse? you ask. Having to explain to my parents why I had to leave after exactly two hours and fifteen minutes—because it took me fifteen minutes to get there, fifteen minutes to get home, and fifteen minutes just to be safe. I never told them why, exactly, I had to limit our time, only that Adder wanted me home because we had plans. Every. Single. Month.

And back in my lockdown, the rules continued. I wish I could say the limits on visiting my parents were the only rules by which I abided, but they weren't. If I got the mail and placed it in the wrong spot on the counter, we would have a fight. If there were other children at the house playing with our children and they forgot to put away their toys, there would be a fight. If dinner was not prepared at a certain time, there would be a fight. I lived by an unwritten manifesto that was laced with fear.

It was a miserable life with a lot of shouting and a lot of name-calling, from him that is. I learned that I would never be anything without him. I was stupid. I was unworthy. I was nothing.

Because I was not allowed to work, even though I had a college degree, it was my job to keep the house immaculate. My days consisted of taking the children to school, going to the gym, cooking, and cleaning the house. In the beginning, if I was lucky, I could sneak off to visit a friend or go for a drive. But I think he started to catch on that I was doing things outside of the house without him because one day when he came home, the first words out of his mouth were "Did you clean today?" and it wasn't in an acknowledging, kind way.

"Of course I did."

"You cleaned everything?"

"Yes, I cleaned everything. I always clean everything. That's all I ever do."

"Mm. Did you sweep and mop?" he asked with a sort of sneer on his face.

"Of course."

He walked over to a corner in the living room, picked up a couple of hairs, and said, "Oh, did you? I thought you cleaned today?"

"I did clean today," I said.

He walked back over to me and threw the hairs in my face.

"I thought you cleaned today," he said, but this time it was not a question.

"I did."

"Then what the fuck are those?" he asked. "Why are those there?"

"I don't know," I said, trying to slowly move backward, afraid he would strike me.

"I put those there last night to see if you really cleaned every corner of this house, you lying bitch. So tell me, why are those there?"

What I wanted to say—no, scream—was "It's a forty-five-hundred-square-fucking-foot house, Adder. I'm sorry if I missed one tiny corner." But I didn't. I looked down, hoping that if he struck me, it would be less of a blow to the main parts of my face and would hit me on the side.

"I'm sorry," I said.

When the kids both finally enrolled in school, I told Adder that I wanted to go back to school for my MBA.

"The kids are both in school and all I'm doing is sitting around the house because I clean so quickly now," I would plead. "You won't let me see my family, so what do you want me to do? Sit here and stare at the walls? I already have my bachelor's in finance, which you know I can't do anything with because I have no work experience, thanks to you. C'mon, please!"

After a few weeks of intense begging sessions and subtle nudges, Adder finally cracked and said yes. When I finally enrolled, we learned that the courses were night classes only, which I think created a lot of insecurities for him and, of course, led to more stress for me. I could tell that he was stressed out and afraid of what I was doing out at night, but what I never understood was that if I wanted to do something wrong, I could do it any time of the day because he was always at work during the day.

When I would come home from my night classes, he would be either upset or in a rage because he had come home from work and had to heat up the dinner and put the kids to bed. And the more I experienced freedom outside of that prison, the more fed up I became with his behavior, the more upset I became because I wanted my daughter to see how a real man treated his wife. I wanted my daughter to see what being a real woman was like. I wanted her to see me as powerful because I knew one day she would be powerful and she would need inspiration to be a boss. I wanted my son to have a good example of how he should treat his future wife. I never wanted him to think that the way Adder behaved was OK.

Because of my extracurriculars, tensions rose in the house; fear was the default emotion. I was terrified of being in that house. I was afraid of what he would do to me. If I was watching the television and my back faced the hallway and I heard any subtle movement, I would jump out of fear. Was he hovering behind me with a gun? Would he suddenly experience a fit of rage and try to strike me? But I will say that throughout all of his anger, in all of his fits of rage, surprisingly, he never physically hit me. But then I start to wonder—was that all part of the trick? Was he too smart to leave evidence? Was it all just some psychological game that couldn't be proven? It's all shocking because with his temper, I never knew when he would snap.

———

Every year Adder was given the top producer award at his company, which meant we got to go on trips once a year— Prague, Italy, Cabo San Lucas. And each time we would go, we would extend our stay and make a vacation out of it for the kids. That year the trip was to the Caymans. Part of me, as usual, was thrilled that I would get to visit what was, in my mind, an exotic place, but the other part of me dreaded it because by the end, I would still be me, and I would still be stuck in that horrible marriage. We stayed at the Ritz-Carlton, and the kids were thrilled.

"We're going to take the kids to this butterfly farm today," Adder said one day. "What do you think?" He passed me a brochure with pictures of people smiling and laughing while butterflies flurried around them. I love butterflies, don't get me wrong, but the thought of them getting stuck in my hair and touching me all over freaked me out, so I asked if I could stay back and hang out on the beach. The sun was high—as it always was—and the gentleman at the front desk said that the water should be the perfect temperature.

I walked through those massive, luxurious doors, past all the cabanas and beautiful young people by the pool, and down into the sand. I escaped from my sandals, leaving them behind, and walked right into the water, the only thought on my mind *This is the most beautiful place I have ever seen.* I had been so many places, seen so many things, but being there—without him—was like being in heaven. The crystal-clear water crashed against my legs, and the shawl hung loose from my shoulders. I daydreamed of my children—only my children—galloping through swarms of butterflies, smiles on their faces, and cute chuckles and teasing. The water splashed me, and I absorbed the beauty that God had given me, had given us. I looked around at the happy couples. There were couples sunbathing, some wading in the water. How could you be unhappy in this paradise on earth?

But I was. I was unhappy, and I was sad. How could I have been in the most amazing place on earth, in one of the most luxurious hotels, with the most beautiful scenery, yet still been sad? In reality, I could have had anything I ever wanted in regard to material possessions, and I was lucky in that sense. All my basic rights as a person had been stripped away, and although sometimes I would trick myself, the money didn't fill that void. If I called out to a bellboy, I could have him bring me all the margaritas I ever desired. I could buy all the clothes I fancied. I could live the lifestyle I had always dreamed of, but I wanted none of it. All I could think in that moment was how much I didn't want to be there. I didn't want to be with him. I didn't want anything except to be with my kids in freedom.

On the flight back home, I decided it was time to file for divorce. I felt empty.

———— •◆• ————

The day after we got home, I dropped the kids off at school and went to an attorney's office, full of fear that perhaps he would somehow track me. I saw people have their vehicles tracked in the movies. With all the money that we had—that he had—it was not out of the realm of possibility that he would know my every move, especially because he knew of my history of sneaking out.

It's funny, after I made the decision on the plane to divorce him, suddenly my life was filled with clarity. Every time I looked at him, I was filled with disgust. When I watched his mouth move, I could only focus on how much I didn't like him. I hated every word that came out of his mouth. I became frustrated with myself for ever being with a man like him. I would watch him eat potato chips and be disgusted by the way he ate them, even though there really was nothing different. Even when he walked out of the door for work, I hated the way that he walked. I didn't want to be near him in any shape or form, which made the sex so much worse. The sex was never good, but is the sex ever good with someone you despise? And from that point forward, it was difficult to stop the tears.

My mantra became "Just get through this." I didn't want him to think there was something going on. I kept things as normal as possible, suffered through the day-to-day, just to get everything over with. I knew that my time was coming and until then it was my responsibility to survive, to help my children survive. I was going to get us out of there. They were my priority.

—•—

The attorney's office was warm, and she looked like an angel to me. I sat across from her desk with anxiety, ready to finally get the help I needed.

"It's best to leave while he's not in the house, maybe while he's at work," she said, "because he's clearly not the type to let you leave willingly with the kids. He's made that threat before, and we're not risking that. I will not let this get ugly."

"He's going to Vegas with friends for a couple of days next week," I said.

"Perfect. You'll leave then. And on the day you leave, you are entitled to take half of everything in your bank account because who knows when he's going to give you money to survive on by the time we go to court. Take half, and keep it moving."

So I started packing my car in small loads while everyone was asleep and taking my belongings to my parents' house. I didn't take much, just a few loads over the course of a few days and mostly stuff for the kids and my clothes. I made sure to grab my photo albums and other objects that held small memories. I took some basic materials like plates and utensils because I knew that I would be starting over and I would need something. Because of the short leash that he kept me on, I had little to no money. I had no clue how I was going to survive, how I would keep my kids alive, but I knew that if I didn't leave, the risk of not being alive would become much bigger.

I called the bank to see how much money I would be able to walk away with, and there was only $8,000. How was I supposed to live off $4,000? How was I supposed to feed the kids? Adder told me that there was a big commission check that was supposed to hit his account in the next few days and that when he returned, we'd celebrate. I could only hope that when the day came to leave, that check would be there. He had a lot of other accounts, investments and insurances but I was not on those accounts so I couldn't touch those.

The next morning we both sat in the kitchen sipping our morning coffee. The open window allowed a chilly breeze to occasionally sweep through the house. It was dark out still, and our house was quiet. Even the kids, for the first time in what felt like forever, were quiet.

"Ready for your trip?" I asked.

His "sure" was spoken so low that I could hardly hear him. I set my coffee down and walked toward the kids' room to pretend to clean up. Even in what was promising to be our last moment together, all I wanted was to get away from him. Don't you want to savor this last moment? I thought. No, not even.

I waited in Jaeda's room for maybe ten minutes before I realized how suspicious my lack of presence would look, so I went back out to the kitchen.

"Don't forget we'll be celebrating when I get back," Adder said.

"OK," I said, knowing that if all went well, we would never celebrate.

On the day Adder was to return, I put the kids in the car and left. We drove immediately to my parents' house, and when we pulled into their driveway, I cried lightly. My hands were shaking, my heart throbbing. I was so scared. I rushed the kids inside and called the bank.

"I need to check my balance," I said.

The teller asked for my details and then told me that there was $250,000 in the account.

The check hit, I thought. The check hit! I couldn't believe it. Someone was looking out for me up there.

"Thank you." I tried to say as calmly as possible. I drove straight down to the bank and requested a cashier's check for half of the balance. When I got back to my parent's house, I moved my car into the garage and ran inside. I called the Duarte police station to let them know what was going on, just in case.

<hr/>

I made sure that the kids and I left the morning he was to come back from Vegas and that he was served with papers when he came back. It didn't take him long to call me, and the first words out of his mouth were "Is there someone else?"

He couldn't even fathom the possibility that maybe the reason I left was him. How could he not have seen how our marriage was going? Had he been absent from our marriage? None of it made sense, and I was confused by his confusion. I replied honestly and said that it was not someone else, that rather, I was not happy and our relationship just was not going to work. He said that he and his friends were going to come by my parents' house the next day to make things right. And I hung up the phone.

And they did show up the next day, just so he could apologize to my parents. Finally, the apology that my parents had waited eight years for. Sadness welled up deep inside of me, but I refused to let it show because as rewarding as it was to finally have my parents get the apology they deserved, the timing was not lost on me. How convenient that the moment I finally decide to leave him and express my unhappiness, he cracks and apologizes. It was tough to even be in the room when it happened, so I sat close to my father. The smallest creak of the house or tap of someone's foot still scared me. Did he expect me to go home with him? Did he expect this apology to fix eight years of misery? Too much had happened, and it had lasted for far too long. He started crying at one point, and all I could think was No, *you* don't deserve to cry. I think for him they were real feelings, albeit psychopathic and narcissistic feelings, but feelings nonetheless. I think in his mind, he really did love me; in his own way, he thought he loved me, but even if he did, it wasn't a healthy love. It was controlling. It was obsessive.

I'm not sure if I did the right thing in that moment. In the same breath, I'm not sure if I did the wrong thing. But in that moment, my initial instinct, after years of manipulative and psychological abuse, was to say, "Fine, for the sake of the kids, maybe I can try to hang in there and stand by my man." Part of me was tempted to succumb like I had for years and years and years. But then my mom stepped in and pulled me into another room.

"He just wants you back, Maia," she said.

"He doesn't get to have you back. He had his chance. He had eight years of chances. Not this time." She paused, seemingly to suppress rage. "You go back with him, Maia, and you won't come back. Mark my words." She came face-to-face with me, her breath on my nose, and whispered, "He knows that you've gone this far, and you think going back with him is safe? Don't even think about it."

She turned and went back to the couch in the living room, crossing her arms and looking at nothing in particular. And that scared the hell out of me. In that moment I decided against returning. Everything about our post-marriage relationship was out in the open now, and I was afraid. But I felt so damn strong.

The weight of the world really hit me a few weeks into living with my parents. I was still in school working on my MBA. Although I had the money I took from our bank account, finances were tight, and I worried about supporting the kids without job security.

I was eager to find a place for the kids so we could have our own little place together. During this time Adder was reluctantly paying child support, as he did until maybe a year into the divorce. Then he suddenly took me back to court and got his child support payments lowered from approximately $11,000 per month to $3,500 per month, stating to the court that he was severely affected due to the 2008 market crash. What I found most peculiar was that his living conditions never really changed. He said his income dropped from $600,000 a year to $150,000 a year, yet he still lived in a 4,500-square-foot home, paid for the kids' private school tuition, drove three fancy cars, went on vacations. And he couldn't pay more to support his own children? Unfortunately, the courts don't use common sense, so despite my pointing this out, nothing ever changed and the truth was never revealed. Adder suddenly stopped getting the top producer awards at his job, and strangely enough, his sister became the top producer. It was funny and suspicious to me that the 2008 market crash only affected him—a veteran in the industry of twenty years—and didn't affect his sister, who had literally just started.

About six months after the initial lowering of child support, Adder took me back to court for a professional assessment, which just meant that the court would evaluate how much I was qualified to make in the workforce. I wasn't working because I was at school full-time trying to earn a degree that would enable me to not even need child support, but the courts didn't see it that way. They evaluated me to be completely capable of working but to have chosen not to, which lowered his child support payment to $1,300 per month. When child support is first discussed with your attorney, the first thing out of their mouth is that he is obligated to keep you and the children at the same standard of living. Well, I'm sure I am not the only person who calls bullshit on that one!

A dear friend of mine, Olivia, had also gone through a divorce at the same time and was experiencing the same financial struggles, so we decided that she would move into our house with her family and we would split expenses. Olivia had a job cleaning houses at the time. Somehow her boss got a contract to help renovate 7-Elevens across the area. He needed people who could go in and clean the stores top to bottom—shelves, refrigerators, you name it—so she asked if I wanted in. At that point I would have taken anything.

Living with Olivia was such a refreshing change of pace, no matter how strapped for money we were. Because at the end of the day, nothing compares to being able to have fun, to living a lighter lifestyle in which you aren't constantly being controlled. We lived together for two years, and it was two years of fun, shenanigans, and most importantly love. Olivia's kids were a little bit older than mine, so they always had a friend around. Even though the adults were constantly working, we found the joy of life in every other moment.

And when the kids wanted money that we never really had to give, we would have them do chores around the house. Our yard was small, but I'll never forget how we told the kids that if they wanted to do chores for money, they would have to go out and cut the grass. We didn't have a lawn mower, though, so the kids went out with a pair of scissors and cut our tiny yard for five dollars, which was an enormous sum for them, so they cut a few patches. Even though spending five dollars on a Happy Meal for the kids was like going to the Ritz-Carlton, and even though we were just barely scraping by, I wouldn't have traded that life for anything. This newfound freedom, although somewhat surreal, was still greater than ever living in that prison. Knowing that my children no longer had a bad influence let me sleep a little lighter at night.

Working at an investment firm as a financial adviser was tough because I still had to take all of my investment licenses and study, which meant that there was very little I could do for the company to earn enough to cover all of our expenses. Although I acknowledged the importance of my parents' help in getting me out of my relationship, I still had a personal issue with constantly asking them for money. Finally, after years of not being free, I wanted to prove not just to myself and to my children but also to the world that I could make it on my own and take care of my own children on my own. So it was back to Olivia's job offer.

"Well, it pays ten dollars an hour ," she said, and I almost hit the floor. Ten whole dollars an hour? I'm going to make bank, I thought.

The gig was always at night, which made studying for school and working at the firm a little bit easier. I would work at the firm and take classes during the day, take care of the kids in the evening when they would come home from school, put them in bed while my brother babysat, and go to work from 9:00 p.m. to 6:00 a.m. The 7-Elevens were mostly in areas of town that I never wanted to be during those hours. And there I sat—on hands and knees, nearly all hours of the night, scrubbing. If my parents had ever found out, they wouldn't have let me keep working there because they knew I was capable of more. They knew that they could just loan me money until I was stable. But it wasn't about the "glamour" of the job, and it certainly wasn't all about the money. It was about making it on my own. I needed to do this for me. I needed to do this for my kids.

When I came home in the mornings after 6:00 a.m., I would get the kids ready for school and take them, go back home and sleep for two hours, wake up, study from noon to 2:00 p.m., pick the kids up, help them do their homework, feed them, be a parent, put them to bed, and head to work. Repeat.

One evening, while preparing some mac and cheese for the kids, my hands started to shake. They had been trembling a few hours before, but I hadn't thought much of it. When they started full-on shaking, I put the pot down and went to the restroom. What the hell is going on with me? I wondered.

My body was finally giving up due to all of the exhaustion, and I was terrified. But I couldn't slow down. I needed to be a mother.

I was studying for my Series 66 and Series 7 at the time, so I always took note cards with me to study while I cleaned. It was productive, and I thought I was clever. Anytime we got a break, I would pull them out and study.

One evening, after an exhausting day at a rigorous class and shenanigans with the kids, I must have been so tired that I was moving slower than normal and less aware of my surroundings because my boss seemed to have snuck up on me.

"What are those?" he asked, pointing at my note cards.

"I'm studying for my investment license. I'm so sorry," I said, shuffling my cards away. I figured the only way to get out of this mess was to explain and pray to God for a little empathy. "I'm in the middle of my MBA program and working during the day as an adviser. You know, single mom just trying to scrape by, trying to make somebody out of myself so I can provide for my kids."

"So you have a college degree?" he asked.

"Yes. I have a bachelor's in finance."

He said nothing but looked shocked, so I said, "I'm so sorry. I'll put them away."

"Get up and come with me."

Par for the course, I did as I was told. He walked me over to the office and said that he was making me a supervisor.

"All you have to do is make sure everyone does their cleaning, understand?"

I nodded yes.

"That way you'll have more time to study your cards," he said, "and, you know, make somebody out of yourself.

Supervisors make five extra dollars, which should help you scrape by a little better. Sound good?"

Perfect.

I passed my test with flying colors the first time I took it. I was finally pulling up for my family, and I couldn't have been prouder.

CHAPTER 5

Starting Over

*When a toxic person can no longer control
you, they will try to control how others see
you. The misinformation will feel unfair, but
stay above it, trusting that other people
will see the truth just like you did.*
—Unknown

The thing about being divorced with kids is that if there is
any sort of shared custody, then there still must be a relationship between the parents. And I wanted us to have a cordial
relationship. His birthday was coming up, so I wanted to buy
him a gift to let him know that I still cared about him as a
human, no matter what we had gone through and no matter
how much I never wanted to be with him romantically again.
I took the kids over to Nordstrom so they could pick out presents for him. They decided on a light-blue dress shirt and tie.

In front of the kids, Adder opened up my trunk, threw the
gift in, and slammed the trunk shut.

"I don't want anything from you."

"Well, it's not from me," I said. "Your kids picked it out."

"Whatever," he said. "I don't want it."

And he walked away back into the house.

On the kids' first day of school that year, we all went as a family to drop them off. As we walked in, the kids walking slightly in front of us, Adder turned to me in front of all of the other parents and said, "Why are you here trying to act like you're a loving mother? Why are you here in front of everybody pretending to be someone you're not?"

I'll forever be grateful that our kids were so young that they didn't realize what was going on. They kept walking and didn't notice, but the other parents did. I was mortified. Why would he treat me this way in front of all of the other parents? What did I do to him? So I did the only thing that I knew how to do based on my life of living within confines—I ignored the hurtful comment and kept walking.

I was the parent who suggested that *we* do a movie night or some sort of outing once a month, to make sure that the children knew that *we* were both still their parents and that *we* both loved them very much. I wanted them to see that we were not enemies and that living with divorced parents could be an amiable experience. I wanted us to be able to go to the park together or visit a museum. I wanted them to see us as normal.

I posed the idea to Adder one day, and he said, "Absolutely not. That's not happening."

"But don't you think it would make our children's lives easier?"

"Maia, I want nothing to do with you. Nothing."

I was shocked but not surprised.

"OK," I said. "I understand."

The long-term goal was to support my children without any outside assistance. I didn't want to be a mother who relied on child support, so I knew that in order to get there, I had to stop working at 7-Eleven so I could focus completely on getting a bigger paycheck. At the beginning I was petrified as I didn't think I would make a good adviser. When I was with Adder, I watched him make proposals and give presentations. The way he would talk seemed impeccable and flawless. And at the time, I was a person without a voice, without a personality, because Adder had kept me under such strict restrictions. I effectively didn't know who I was, so the thought of presenting in front of people and pretending as if I knew who I was seemed impossible.

In the months and years that I had been out of my relationship with Adder, I had started to finally—for the first time in my life—discover who I truly was, what my values were, what my morals were. I became more outgoing than introverted, more affable than shy.

During my first few appointments with clients and potential clients, I constantly had to remind myself that those people didn't know me; they didn't know the person I used to be, so I could behave any way I wanted to. I could be whomever I wanted. In essence, I gave myself the courage to be human, to be myself, to own my knowledge and my freedom.

Every year in June there is a massive jewelry show in Vegas that all of the big-time jewelers go to. Because my parents were in the industry and were decently successful and because my brothers always joined my parents, I decided to go too. One evening after the show, I stopped at the hotel bar for a drink to unwind. The basketball playoffs were on, so we sat there for hours watching and drinking and being siblings, and it was moments like those when I felt so incredibly grateful because it seemed as if I had been given another opportunity to relive moments with my brothers—all the moments I never got to have. When we were young, the only thing I could think of was how afraid I was of Adder. There was always a distractor taking my conscious away from the present. And finally, after years, we were allowed to be just that—siblings.

From the corner of my eye, I could see this broad-shouldered gentleman approaching our high-top. He had a luscious beard, and I was immediately attracted to him.

My brothers Drew and Toby didn't speak much; they only gave snarky side-eyes to each other and interjected to make quips.

Eventually David and I shared our numbers, and my heart was on cloud nine. This type of chance encounter was exactly what I had dreamed of since I was in college. I had dreamed of being free to love. And here it was.

"What are you doing?" Toby asked.

"What do you mean?"

"You can't actually talk to that guy. The only guy you should be talking to is God," he joked.

I gave a fake chuckle and pointed back to the playoffs. I was over letting men control my life, but I respected Toby, so I let it slide. It was clear that he had no issue with David hitting on random women, but for me—a woman—to engage? Blasphemous. That's Syrian culture, baby.

I didn't expect to ever hear from David again, so when I got back home to California to find a voicemail, I was shocked. I called him back that evening.

"So where do you live in Vegas?" he asked.

"Oh," I said, "I actually live in California. In Los Angeles."

There was a pause, and my heart sank. I should have known this was coming.

"All right, well, I want to drive up to see you."

I hadn't expected a man to drive three-and-a-half hours to come visit *me* of all people, so I said OK.

A few days later, he called again and said he was going to come up on the weekend and asked for my address.

How can I put this delicately—my initial reaction, as crass as it may be, was a simple one: What the fuck?

"I'm going on a trip up there anyway, so I figured I'd stop in and see your gorgeous face. That's OK, isn't it?"

Here was a handsome man I was so attracted to, who seemed like such an incredible person, who had actually made an effort to come visit me.

That chance encounter blossomed into a real relationship. My very first "real" relationship. One I chose to be in because I wanted to, not because I felt I had to. Around Halloween of that year, David and I decided that it was time to introduce him to my kids and introduce me to his daughter, Amanda. I was nervous about how my kids would handle another man around, so we initially introduced him as just my friend. His daughter was gorgeous, with beautiful blond hair and the bluest eyes. She was only two, but she spoke as if she were five.

And thankfully my children took to Amanda so quickly. They thought she was so fascinating and followed her around the house wherever she went. They had a new friend, a new source of joy, and as a mother, it made my heart so happy.

As for David, they adored him. He behaved exactly how I wanted a boyfriend to behave—like a father. He would play with them, speak to them with love and care, and express genuine interest in getting to know them, even though they were so young.

I really liked David. He was the all-American guy. You know, so much fun and lighthearted. We would watch football games together. We would play golf even though I didn't and still don't play golf. I was in charge of driving the golf cart, and we had so much fun on those courses. He was great with the kids and even loved them.

I saw a future with him at that six-month mark, which is why I decided to introduce him to my kids; I wanted to see where it would go. I started taking the kids to see him once a month. It was a three-and-a-half-hour drive to David's house, and we would make it a special occasion. The kids would bring snacks, and we would play car games. They loved going to see their new friend Amanda, and I loved spending time with David, especially with my kids around. The room was always so full of love, and he always kept us entertained.

I have to give it to my kids—they're brilliant, so I should have known that they would realize David and I were more than friends pretty quickly. In December they started to hint at it by poking fun at us, saying that we spent a lot of time together and mentioning the way he looked at me. I also should have known that all good things must come to an end, by which I mean it was only a matter of time before their father found out that I was in a happy relationship.

The kids had a fundraiser at school in which they had to accept donations based on how many laps they were to run in a marathon. The donator was to put their money in an envelope and write their name and how much they donated on the envelope. David donated twenty dollars and wrote his name down on the envelope. When the children took this sheet to their father for donations, he must have seen David's name right next to mine in the same handwriting with the same dates.

When the kids brought the envelope back to me, David's name was completely crossed off with Adder's name directly underneath it. For a moment I was right back in that terrible marriage. A massive wave of fear overcame me, as if I would be in trouble with him for doing something I shouldn't have done. I was afraid that he would come barreling through that door with a gun and scream at me for being with another man. In that moment I completely forgot where I was, and that scared the hell out of me. And it was only a matter of time until things escalated.

But that didn't stop us. Eventually David and I had gotten pretty serious. His house was too small to fit all of us comfortably, so we decided to rent a house down there for when we visited—a house with enough beds and enough room for the kids to have fun. The girls had a bedroom with bunk beds, which they loved, and Aden got his own room. We spent a lot of money decorating it so that the kids would be as comfortable as possible. Even though we rented the house so David and I could see each other more often while still bringing the loves of our lives, the trips really became about intermingling our families. And decorating that house with the sole intention of making it comfortable for our kids made it seem as if my heart was exploding sometimes. I was overfilled with joy and love and found myself crying while picking out furniture or paint swabs. This was going to be our new home, and I was simply happy. It was our home away from home, and it became our safe haven.

Someone once asked me if I was shocked to meet a man who was so normal after decades of being in a relationship with someone who was so unhealthy. My answer was a quick and simple one—no. Despite how much I had gone through, I was—and still am—a hopeless romantic. I believe in love. I believe in true love. I believe in real love. And I love love.

When I was growing up, my mom would always recruit me to help in the kitchen. If I could, I'd write an entire book about the meals we'd make and the time we spent making them. Naturally, when I became a mother, I wanted the same for my children. Although they weren't as quick to help, we would still help each other out. The kids' favorite dish was skinny spaghetti noodles with ground beef, tomato sauce, and onions. It was so simple—forty-five minutes at five-hundred degrees—but they thought it was heaven.

One evening we were all in the kitchen and dining room preparing the infamous spaghetti.

Aden had finished putting the forks on the table when I placed the spaghetti down.

"Hey, Mom?" Aden asked.

"Yes?"

"If we were stranded on a boat and you could only save two people, would you save me, Amanda, or Jaeda?"

Jaeda and Amanda looked at each other, and I laughed.

"What a silly question," I said. "I would save all of you."

"You can only save two."

"Well, it wouldn't stop me from trying. And I'm sure David would help. Wouldn't you?" I asked, looking at him.

He laughed and jokingly said, "Depends on how good you've all been lately. Put your napkins on your laps."

I served the spaghetti and asked Aden how his day was.

"I'm serious," he said.

"Honey, why are you asking me this?"

"Just answer, Mom."

"I'm serious. I'd save all of you. I love you all so much."

I was deeply concerned by this question because it wasn't like Aden to ask questions like this, let alone speak that way. It didn't sound like him, and I was afraid.

A few days later, Jaeda came to me saying that their dad told them having a stepdad is bad because stepdads are mean.

"Why would he say that to you?" I asked.

"I don't know," she said.

"You don't even have a stepfather. David and I are just dating for now. And you know David, right?"

"Yes."

"And you know how nice he is, right?"

"Uh-huh."

"Then you have nothing to worry about. I would never let anyone be mean to you or Aden."

⚊⚫⚊

As we loaded up the car one weekend to drive to David's, Jaeda and Aden both started complaining about going.

"What do you mean?" I asked. "You love going and playing with Amanda."

"We did," Aden said.

"But you've been talking about it all week?"

Silence.

We still went that weekend because the plans were already made, and the kids had fun when they got there, but something had changed. Suddenly they were against going to visit, and I was concerned.

———— ◆ ————

I was certain the complaints about Vegas were a result of some phase they were going through—growing pains, perhaps. You know, I thought, maybe it would make them feel better if they saw me and David attend Palm Sunday together—an extremely important day in our house. The preparations included picking out clothes, deciding on a meal, and determining with whom we would spend the day.

That warm Los Angeles sun beat down on us, causing the kids to complain about the heat, but my God, did we look fine. I always let them have fun with their outfits for church, so long as they kept it decent. I was grateful that they were with me that Palm Sunday weekend, but I knew that because it was Palm Sunday, Adder would probably show up to our church so he could see them too. I knew the chance was high, but I wasn't going to let him stop me from enjoying this beautiful and important day with my children and my boyfriend.

We arrived with my family and mingled outside of the church, eventually making our way inside to escape the heat. We found our seats and mingled with the folks around us.

During the service, I felt someone staring at me. I've always found it odd how we can sense those sorts of things, especially when the stare is not well-intentioned. I looked over, and of course it was Adder. Why was I surprised? I knew this sort of thing was going to happen. I said nothing to David.

At the end of the service, Adder made himself visible to the kids, so of course they ran over to say hi. David and I stayed back. Eventually the kids came back over to me, and I felt this unusual sense of gratitude. Unusual in the sense of *I hope and pray that for all my life, if my kids ever wander off, they will always return to me.* It was something I had never really thought of before, and it scared me that I was even having that thought. We left promptly to avoid an interaction.

The next day I received the first email. It was from Adder, and it was about how poor a mother I was. It was in a tone that I had noticed hints of before, but never with such intensity. I can't even bring myself to repeat most of what it said, but the gist was that I was an unfit mother, a whore, that I didn't care about my kids—only David and Amanda. He said that I was torturing the kids by constantly taking them to Vegas and that I should be ashamed of myself. After I read it, I sobbed for hours. How could someone say such untrue and hurtful things? And it was David who reminded me that just because it was in writing didn't mean it was true. I loved my kids more than anything in the world, to the point that if they had told me they hated David, I would have left him. It would have been as simple as that. Then I thought, constantly taking them to Vegas? We go once a month for three days.

Valerie, my bestie, was such a saint, consoling me for the next week. She pointed out that the kids had no issue with going to Vegas until the week that Jaeda said Adder told her stepdads were bad. Her comment opened my eyes; I would now pay closer attention to the comments the kids made and the changed behavior after those comments.

———— ◆ ————

The kids spent Christmas with their dad that year, so I decided to spend the week with David in Vegas. Christmas evening, we went out to the Eiffel Tower for dinner and strolled the Strip. We eventually made our way to the Venetian, where they had gondolas out on the river around the hotel. David suggested we take one of the gondolas for a romantic trip, so of course I said yes. He held my hand as I entered the gondola, like the perfect gentleman. As our gondola was led through the water, we cuddled and watched the lights pass us by, with the gentle sound of water rippling around the boat. Italian music played off in the distance as the sun set. I couldn't have been happier.

"You know," David said, "I really love you."

"I know," I said, grinning.

"No, I mean it. I really, really love you."

"OK," I said, wondering where this was going.

He maneuvered so he could face me, and he knelt down off the bench. It was naturally an awkward position, but he clearly was so comfortable.

"And, Maia, will you marry me?" he said, pulling out a ring.

My jaw hit the floor of the gondola. For the first time in my life, I was speechless.

I said yes almost instantly. This was truly the ultimate Christmas gift.

When we got home, I called my parents and they congratulated me. I was still in shock. I was so thrilled, and I missed my kids terribly.

About a week or two later, David received an email.

It more or less read "Back off." Adder said that David would never be Aden's dad and that if he ever hurt Jaeda again, he'd kill him. "Wait a minute," we both said, "*again*?" David had never been around the kids without me, so what did he mean?

"Maybe he means the Super Bowl party?" David wondered.

Ah yes, the Super Bowl party. Jaeda and David were roughhousing—which she loved. She was a total tomboy who loved to play-wrestle.

"That must have been it," I said. "He's lost his mind!"

David was a big guy, so Jaeda loved to jump on his back and sneak attack him. I remember her leg getting caught when he went to flip her over onto the couch and her saying, "Whoa, whoa, whoa" to let him know she was stuck. He put her down immediately and apologized, and they both laughed.

"And now I abused her, right?" David asked, and we both looked at each other in total dismay.

And then I received an email.

"If he ever laid a finger on my daughter…"

My daughter, he said. In that moment he tried to take my daughter away from me, and it enraged me. To the point it became comical. I was her mother. How could he even think that he could possess her—our gorgeous daughter—with his words? I wouldn't allow it. Did he really think that I would sit there and watch someone abuse my child?

A few days later, I decided that there wasn't going to be any more roughhousing. I couldn't afford for there to be any more accusations, let alone for one of my children to accidentally trip and scrape their knee. Suddenly I was in protective mama bear mode, and I was so scared. I let David know when we first got together that I had a crazy ex and that if it bothered him, he didn't need to be with me.

"If you're down to push through this with me, then great," I said, "but if this is something you don't want to deal with, then let me know now."

I expected him to either walk out the door in that moment or play it off as if he was OK with it but then later suddenly disappear. But he didn't.

"I don't care, Maia," he said. "We all have our own shit. We're human."

And then he told me about his crazy ex.

"We can survive our crazy exes together. How's that sound?" he asked.

I just smiled. That sounded perfect.

———

We were cooking dinner as a family, laughing and playing around. Everyone had a responsibility, and we were happy. It was a gorgeous Thursday California evening. Then there was a knock on the door, so I walked over to answer it.

"Hello, ma'am." There were two police officers and they looked concerned.

"Can I help you?" I asked, worried.

"Are you Maia Amin?"

"Yes. What's going on?"

"We got a call regarding abuse," one officer said.

"Abuse? Are you sure you have the right house?" I asked as the kids laughed in the background while making their dinner.

"We're sure. We just need to check on the kids in the house, if that's all right?"

"Of course, but we're making dinner. I mean, you can hear them laughing, right?"

"Yes, ma'am. This is just routine. If there's no abuse, you have nothing to worry about," he said, walking past me.

"What's going on?" David asked as the officers and I entered the kitchen.

"The officers here just have to ask us some questions because there's been some report of abuse," I said, still beyond confused.

"Hey, kids," the other officer said happily, "we're going to talk to you all. Is that OK?"

The kids looked as confused as I was, but all nodded yes.

The officers took the kids into separate rooms, and David and I speculated about the cause.

"Do you really think he'd do something like this?" David asked, alluding to Adder.

"Of course he would."

Eventually the police returned and told us that there was no sign of abuse and even acknowledged how fun our house was, how put together it was.

"Listen," the officer said, "we visit a lot of homes for this reason, so to find a home like this, it makes us sleep better at night."

I told them that I thought it was my ex-husband's way of expressing his sorrow and anger at me meeting a new man.

"It's not uncommon for an ex-spouse to lodge a complaint so they have a paper trail," the officer said. "We'll give you a citation number so you can have that for your records, and it'll note that we found nothing and that your house is actually in great condition, as are its occupants."

When the officers left, I asked the kids how their conversations went, and they said the cops directly asked if they were abused.

"And what did you say?"

"We said, you know, no, you don't, but sometimes."

"Sometimes?"

"Well yeah, you know, you tap us on our hands when we're bad, but you're our mom, so you have to."

"You know that's not abuse, though, right?"

"Yeah," Aden said, and Jaeda nodded.

"You know that poking you or tapping you isn't abuse? It's to let you know that you did something wrong or so you can pay attention. If I hit you with a belt or my hand, that would be abuse. 'Abuse' is a big word with serious consequences."

"Yes," Jaeda said.

"So if a cop ever asks you if I abuse you, you tell them the truth."

I explained to them that there are bad parents out there who actually abuse their kids and that I would never do that to them, that I may discipline them but I would never hurt them.

"We're sorry, Mom," Aden said.

"No, it's OK. I just want you to know the difference and that I love you so very much."

The next morning I had a feeling that something was amiss. I still can't explain it, but I knew something was wrong and that trouble was encroaching.

I woke up early and got the kids ready for school. Everything was going fine, and there was a chill in the air.

"Would you mind being nearby the kids' school this morning when I take them in?" I asked David. "I have a feeling Adder might try something."

"Of course, sweetie," he said, leaning over to kiss my forehead.

Because of my uneasy feeling, I played upbeat music on the drive to school and held their hands tightly as I walked them into the building. I wanted them to feel my love through our hands. I smiled like a moron. Kids were jogging to get into the building on time, and parents were rushing up to remind their kids of their forgotten lunches or jackets. I felt at home among the other families. I was happy.

Seemingly out of nowhere, Keres rushed up to us, on the side Jaeda was on, and shouted, "Oh my God, are you OK, Jaeda? Are you OK?"

I looked down at her to see if something had happened that I hadn't noticed. My heart felt like it would explode.

She grabbed Jaeda by the arm, and Jaeda tried to pull away. "Are you OK, my love?"

Other parents stopped and stared, and I was so confused.

Then it hit me—they were trying to make another call to the police.

I examined Jaeda quickly, realized that nothing had changed while her hand was still in mine, and said, "She's fine."

Jaeda unlatched herself from Keres, and we kept walking.

"I just wanted to make sure you weren't still injured," she said.

"Either way, it's none of your business," I said and kept us walking.

Keres grabbed Jaeda again and tried yanking her away from me.

A surge of adrenaline shot through my veins, and I felt like a mama bear.

"Let go of my daughter, *now*," I growled.

I pulled Aden and Jaeda closer, feeling unsafe, and said, "Let's go. We're not staying here." I would return them when the coast was clear, but in that moment, school was not a safe space for my children. We had turned to walk back to the car when I saw Adder come running down the hill beside the school. He stopped in front of us to ask Jaeda, again, if she was OK.

If they were asking Jaeda if she was OK due to the police being called less than twenty-four hours prior, then why didn't they ask Aden if he was OK? I was beyond confused and knew something wasn't right.

"Let's go," I said to the kids again.

"Where are you going?" Adder asked. "It's a school day, and you're not allowed to take them away from school."

"We have a doctor's appointment," I said.

Adder and Keres started tugging at Jaeda, and I started to panic. I managed to pull my phone out of my purse and call David. I told him what was going down and to call 911. I needed to have my hands free to hold on to both of my children.

All the parents were still watching us, and the kids were both crying. Somehow the principals were alerted, and they approached to mediate.

"Let's go to our office to figure this out," the principal said. "We don't want to freak out the parents."

I respected the school and its authority, so I agreed. As we turned around, David came down the hill in a hurry, worried we were being hurt. My heart fluttered at the thought of David caring so much about my kids that he would step in to help. He truly cared.

Adder turned and saw David, then jogged over to him with his middle finger extended. Now, David had an injured eye because of an accident earlier in his life. He was sensitive to that, so I'm sure when Adder came at him with a finger extended, David wasn't comfortable.

Adder shoved David—a 250-pound man—which just hardly budged him. And in the frenzy of the crazy, David—to protect himself—pushed Adder away, making contact with his chest.

Adder clutched his throat, as if David had touched it, dropped to the ground, crying, shouting, "I can't breathe! I can't breathe! He punched me in the throat!"

For a man who said he was punched in the throat and couldn't breathe—despite having never actually been touched there—he did a lot of talking. As the crazy continued, parents panicking, kids crying, Adder shouting, and the principals trying to get a handle on the situation, Adder came up behind me and pinched my back.

"Don't you touch me," I said. "Get your hands off me right now."

He said he didn't touch me, but when I got home, David checked and there was a bruise at the spot—he had pinched me that hard.

When the cops came, Adder said he wanted to press charges against David, but eventually we all came to an agreement because they said if anyone was going to press charges, everyone would have to go downtown and possibly to jail until things were sorted out.

The next day David was notified that Adder had pressed charges and filed for a restraining order.

My entire life was flashing before my eyes, and I was terrified that I was going to lose my children and my fiancé. It felt as if I were watching my life blow up before me, all because of a controlling narcissist.

In court, I'm sure that when the judge took one look at David—the massive man he is—and one look at Adder—a rather skinny, older man—he made a prejudgment.

Keres testified that she saw what happened between David and Adder, even though she didn't. She was well ahead of us, already in the school, when it happened.

Adder's lawyer brought up the Super Bowl incident and the supposedly anonymous report of abuse.

Everything somehow fell in Adder's favor, and the judge issued a three-year restraining order against David, meaning David couldn't come near Adder or my children.

I sobbed for days. David couldn't even return to my home. What were we going to do?

As quickly as it began, it ended. Our love boarded a gondola and I sobbed enough to fill the river so that it could float away.

David and I tried to stay together for a little while after that, but it was mostly long-distance, and it wasn't working. How could he go three years without seeing my kids and still play a major role in my life?

He eventually moved on. We don't speak anymore, but on occasion, I still think about the crazy part of my life he was involved in.

After David was gone, I started to notice quirks in Jaeda and Aden's behavior and communication—patterns that started at the end of my relationship with David. They were reminiscent of the way they suddenly had mixed feelings about David or the way they told the police that I hurt them. They had used negative language about "stepdads," and they had exhibited a lack of emotion toward me.

Now that David was gone, these behaviors usually manifested only when we'd come in contact with Adder in passing. If we were out on the town holding hands and they spotted Adder, they'd drop my hand and cross their arms. If I was waiting at school with them for Adder to come pick them up, as soon as Adder arrived, they'd scootch over and act as if they didn't know me. No goodbye kiss or "I love you." Their lack of affection and emotion toward me scared me, but it was only when *he* was around. It was only a matter of time before this behavior manifested into something else—something scarier, something worse.

One evening in late March, I walked down into my room to think and pray. How was it that I had spent years battling my own inner conscious, years fighting to get myself and my children out of that marriage safely and unscathed, to get them to a safe home, that I fought so hard for my children, and now it seemed like I was losing them? As I sat there and prayed for my children, I also prayed for forgiveness for the way I abandoned my parents when I was young. I knew that it wasn't my fault, that I had been manipulated by this man, but I still felt guilt. I still felt shame. My parents did everything they could to give us better lives. They moved us to America, they kept food on our plates, they bought us clothes. Was it difficult growing up as a Syrian child in America? Of course it was. Was it difficult having Syrian parents who weren't interested in assimilating to American culture? Of course it was. Was it difficult being bullied because of my Syrian culture? Of course it was. But my parents were always there for me. They always looked out for us. They always kept us safe, clean, and healthy. And I abandoned them.

And sitting there on my bed, I realized that I was at a precipice, that my family was at a precipice. Just as I had abandoned my parents for Adder, Jaeda was now abandoning me. But I'll be damned if I was going to let that happen.

CHAPTER 6

Suspiciously Familiar

*When your abuser can no longer control
you, they will try to break you.*
—Unknown

All of a sudden, after David was gone, my work started to pick up. I was making more money than I ever had, and I was finally able to afford the lifestyle that I wanted for my children. I had never really made money before. Just a few years prior, I was scrubbing the floors of 7-Eleven in the most impoverished communities just so we could scrape by. I was so incredibly proud of myself and so thrilled that I was able to properly take care of my children without fear that Adder would not pay his child support.

To celebrate, I decided to take the children on an amazing, unforgettable trip. One of their favorite shows to watch at the time was *Cake Boss*, so the plan was to take them over to Jersey, have them try a cake at the bakery from the show, and then go sightseeing in New York.

About a week before departure, I told them that we were going on a trip but they had to guess where we were going to go. The excitement was so intense that it kept them up at night. Every day they would lodge guesses, and they would be the most outlandish guesses that would keep us laughing for hours. One of them was "Idaho."

I looked at Aden, laughing so hard I thought I was going to pee, and said, "What's in Idaho?"

Aden replied, "Well, the Idaho potatoes, of course."

I laughed even harder. "Yeah, right. We're going to see the Idaho potatoes."

"Mom, stop," Jaeda said. "Where are we really going?"

"You'll have to wait and see."

We laughed some more, and I reveled in the moment.

When we were alone, it was almost as if all of our troubles stayed at bay. There was no interference of Adder and his negativity. It was just my beautiful children and I enjoying each other's presence. Sometimes I would get scared that the moment would be ruined with a weird comment spurred by an idea so clearly planted by Adder. Something like, "Will you ever remarry? Because you know stepdads are mean, right?" or "Would you ever leave us?" These broke my heart because I knew what was going on. And I would combat those thoughts the only way I knew how—with love. I would reassure them about how much I loved them. I would hug them. I would hold their hand. I would tell them that I would die for them. In those moments it took everything not to cry.

On the day of the trip, in August 2014, the children still hadn't properly guessed, but we boarded our first flight. When we boarded the second flight, the children were smart enough to point out that the itinerary said New Jersey.

"What are we doing in New Jersey?" they both screamed in excitement.

"OK, I'll tell you the plan, but I'm not telling you everything because I want it to be a surprise. We're going to see something special in New Jersey, and then we're going to go across the river to New York City and spend a week sightseeing, visiting all the cool things you always talk about—the Statue of Liberty, Central Park, everything."

If I could live in that moment forever, I probably would. They were on cloud nine, smiles from ear to ear. They couldn't believe where we were going, and I could have cried because I, too, was on cloud nine with them.

———◆———

As planned, we went to Carlos's Bakery, and the kids were even more ecstatic than I thought they'd be. They picked out the cake they wanted after some serious deliberation. After pizza for dinner, we went back to our room at the Hyatt in New Jersey to dive into the cake.

A few days later, we met my brother Drew, who had planned to meet us there. The children always had fun with him, and they were so excited that he was with us. On the way to the Statue of Liberty, I tripped and sprained my ankle. I was having a hard time walking around, but absolutely nothing was going to get in the way of us exploring that lovely city. I tried to hide how much I was struggling from the children, but when we got to the statue and they told us how many stairs there were to get to the top, I knew I had to take the elevator. The children were dying to take the stairs up to the top. Normally I would never let them go anywhere alone, but I thought, What's the worst that can happen? They can't get lost because there's only one place they can go—to the top. So I let them. I told them to wait for me when they got up there.

What they don't tell you is that the Statue of Liberty elevator is the slowest elevator in the entire world. I mean, I think I've seen elderly women move faster. When I got to the top, the children were nowhere in sight. Then, over the intercom system, we heard that there were two kids waiting at security for their mom, Maia. For the love of God, I thought. How did this happen? I sent Drew down to the bottom to wait with them until I got there. When I arrived, they looked frightened and came running up to hug me. They said that they thought we had left them.

"Why on earth would we leave you?" I asked.

"I don't know," Jaeda said. "We thought you wanted to get rid of us."

"I would never, ever try to get rid of you two, Jaeda. I love you more than anything."

Where was this coming from? When had I ever abandoned them? *Never* was the simple answer. I was frustrated that they didn't follow my instructions because I knew that this story would get back to Adder and become another alleged incident of abuse and/or negligence.

After that, the trip was pretty normal. We visited the 9/11 memorial, went to the top of the Chrysler Building, visited M&M World (where they purchased the largest gummy worm I've ever seen—at least three feet), and even went to Wall Street. It was a trip to remember, and they slept the entire flight home.

A day after we returned home, they went to be with their father, and everything seemed fine. The entire weekend and the following week, there was nothing out of the ordinary. There were no notices, no calls from Adder ranting about anything. All of a sudden, on Friday, right before it was my weekend with the kids again, I got a call from CPS saying there were allegations of abuse.

"Excuse me?" I said.

The allegations were from a couple of weeks ago, when we were in New York.

It was late on a Friday, and once an allegation had been made, I legally wasn't allowed to pick up the kids until an investigation was conducted. Not to mention that I couldn't even call my lawyer since lawyers don't work weekends.

Wait a minute, I thought. Is this a pattern? It seemed as if every time the children were excited or happy about anything that they did with me, it turned into some sort of incident with Adder. Either it was a CPS report and investigation or some sort of accusation of abuse. I spent more than $10,000 to take my kids to New York just to beat them? It didn't make sense to me. And by the time CPS completed their investigations, I would lose another weekend with the kids. I found it convenient that nearly every CPS investigation occurred when I was supposed to have a weekend with the kids. And every single time I was investigated, CPS found nothing.

After New York, life stayed pretty consistent—CPS reports that not only yielded no findings of abuse but also took my weekends away, work getting better and better, bonding with my kids through fun trips and nights in, and the occasional incident of seeing Adder or his family in public causing the children to become uncomfortable and retreat from me.

Then, in March 2015, things started to get worse.

Jaeda had a party coming up one weekend for her basketball team, but I had told her that if she didn't get her grades up, she couldn't go to the party. I never raised a hand to my children for discipline; instead I chose to use a more effective method to help them grow. She was upset about it, but I don't think she took me seriously. The week of the party, I asked what her grade was, and she said it was still a C. I was shocked. This wasn't like her. She always got straight As. What gives? It broke my heart, but I told her that she couldn't go to the party. I expected annoyance on her end, but there was nothing.

That Friday we stopped at a gas station on the way to school because the kids wanted a special snack. I dropped them off using the drop-off lane at school, and they collected their backpacks, got out, and walked into the school. I went on with the rest of my day, running errands, talking to clients. Then around 1:00 p.m. I got a call from a social worker.

"Is this Maia Amin?"

"Yes, it is," I said.

"We have your daughter here at the school and she's crying hysterically because she said that you hit her."

"*I hit her?*" I said, shocked. "She's been in school all day. How could I have hit her? What are you talking about?"

"Ms. Amin, she said that you hit her this morning when you dropped her off in front of the school."

"And she just remembered now?" I said, almost joking. "If I hit her at eight a.m., then why is she crying now?" There was disapproving silence. "Ma'am, I did not hit my kid. I don't even spank them to discipline them. You can watch the security footage from the school."

"We will," she said. "But right now, she's terrified, and she doesn't want to go home with you tonight, so we're going to honor that."

"Are you serious right now?" This is absurd, I thought. If I wanted to abuse my child—which I never did and still don't to this day—why would I do it in public, in the drop-off lane at their school, for anyone to see? The facts weren't adding up, and I was confused, angry, and sad.

"OK," I said. "What do you suggest? When *can* I get her?"

"Well, I suggest she stay with her father this weekend."

"OK. Wait, so I can still pick up Aden, right?"

There was a pause. "Uh, well, sure. Of course you can."

"So explain something to me, will you? If I'm an abusive parent, why am I allowed to take one child home but not the other?"

There was an even longer pause. I waited.

"It's protocol, ma'am."

Protocol, I thought. Ridiculous.

I was so beyond furious and frustrated. Another weekend to spend with my daughter was gone. I didn't realize the connection between the lie of me hitting her and her basketball party until I saw a picture of her at the party on Facebook. And what does this mean for the future? I thought. If CPS kept investigating to find no proof of abuse, why did no one believe me? Why had my life been uprooted like this? And, God forbid, what would happen if a serious allegation was made? For example, what if one of the kids were to lie and say I pulled a knife on them? I was terrified and in total disbelief.

That following Monday I was told that I could take Jaeda home again. What changed? I wondered. If there was no investigation, no one interviewing me, then what could have possibly changed? Nothing. Suddenly I was deemed a fit mother again—just like that. It was just another baseless accusation, most likely—if I had to guess—planted into my child's mind.

I knew that if I was going to make things right, if I was going to keep my children, something needed to change, so I told CPS that I wasn't going to take Jaeda back until we all started going to therapy. I needed to figure out why she was lying because I no longer felt safe, even with my own children, and I wanted professional help. She had to understand that allegations that serious could have put me in jail. She was at an age where she knew the difference between right and wrong and knew it was not OK to lie. I had requested therapy for more than a year, and Adder had refused to allow it.

I gave this exact scenario to the social worker. I said, "If a child needs therapy and one parent is refusing to give them the help they need, is that not considered negligence? How come you can't do anything about that yet you continue to investigate me on baseless accusations?"

I knew something was going on, and I was going to save my family from whatever it was.

CHAPTER 7

One Last Kiss

Never try to fuck up someone's life with a lie when yours can be destroyed with the truth.
—Unknown

At the beginning, Adder still refused to allow Jaeda to enter therapy. For the next two months, when I would drop Aden off at school or pick him up, we would run into Jaeda and my heart would break. She would try to speak to us, and I would keep it light because I was afraid that another lie of abuse would emerge. Standing my ground—in order to protect us all—was to date the hardest thing I have ever had to do.

One of the times we ran into her, she asked when she was going to be allowed to come home again, and I started to cry.

"I just want to know why you've been lying, Jaeda. I won't be mad, I swear. I just want to know. Because your lies are hurting me. And if they keep happening, then I won't be allowed to be your mother anymore. Why did you tell them I hit you?"

And I'll never forget what she said next. She looked me right in the eyes and said, "Because you did."

All of the blood drained from my face. What was happening? Was there something wrong with her? Was there something wrong with me? Did I hit her and not even remember it? I would never touch my child like that, but if she was so serious—I started to question everything, and suddenly I felt insane. I got chills all over and seriously questioned my sanity. It was the way she looked me dead in the eyes and told me that I had.

Aside from being scared of my child, saying no to my child has been one of the hardest experiences of my life. It made me wonder if I was doing something wrong. Would this give Adder more ammunition in the battle against me? Was I supposed to not acknowledge the lies that could have seriously damaged my life? Was I supposed to let her think it was OK to go through life making allegations about people that were untrue?

The decision to not allow her to come home was, if I had to choose, harder than the decision to leave Adder years earlier. I had to fake the confidence of a mother and constantly remind myself that there would never be a soul who could give me the best answer as to whether or not I made the best or worst decision.

One day in May, after about a month of keeping it cordial, Jaeda, Aden, and I were sitting in the cafeteria waiting for Adder to pick them up. I went to take a selfie with Jaeda. We were smiling and looking cute, and I was dying to commemorate that. We were starting to feel normal again. As soon as we took the picture, Jaeda turned around and then went pale, as if she'd seen a ghost.

"Jaeda, what's wrong?" I asked, and then I saw Adder watching us from across the room.

"Jaeda, what is wrong?"

"I'm fine. It's OK," she said, picked up her bag, and ran toward her father.

From that day on, anytime I would see her at school, she would avoid me. She would hide her face, jog away, whatever she had to do.

Mother's Day was coming up in a few weeks, so I decided to give in. It had been a couple of months since I allowed Jaeda to come home with me, and I missed her more than anything in the world. I didn't know what else to do to remedy this situation, and therapy clearly wasn't going to happen. So the Thursday prior to Mother's Day, I gave in and said that I would pick her up for the weekend.

We ordered Chipotle and played some music. For the first time in months, I felt whole again. I finally had my children back with me, and I had to step away a few times to cry tears of joy. On Thursday evening Jaeda pulled me aside to let me know that she wanted to live with her father.

"Wait a minute, what?" I said.

She was panicked, it seemed like. "No, no," she said. "I'll come back to visit you a lot, it's just that…I want to live with Dad."

She wasn't even thirteen yet. Did she know what that massive, adult decision would even mean for her?

It took me a little while to process what was happening, so we sat down.

Once again it was an internal struggle for me: Should I be more empathetic and listen to my daughter, or should I use my own logic, be the authoritative parent who makes decisions based on what I believe to be the best for her? I truly wanted her to think I was giving her a choice in everything she did in her life, but at the same time, she was a preteen incapable of making adult decisions. If she was going to make an adult decision, she needed to know the consequences. After hours of going back and forth with her crying, yelling, debating, I finally said, "OK. But that doesn't mean I don't get to see you."

"I know," she said. There was a long pause of silence that felt like eternity. How is this even real? I thought.

"Can I go back this weekend?" Jaeda asked.

"But you just got here?"

I was devastated, but what else could I do? What good would come from forcing her to stay at my house? Jaeda said nothing.

"I'll text your father and ask him if he doesn't mind picking you up, and then you can come back for Mother's Day on Sunday," I said. She agreed.

And then the text came. Early Sunday morning I got a text from Adder that said Jaeda didn't want to stay with me for the weekend.

"It's not her choice," I replied. The courts had agreed to this schedule because she was a minor, and the court system in America believes that minors shouldn't make adult decisions, or so I thought.

"I'm coming to get her at noon," I replied.

I dropped Aden off at my parents' house because my instincts, which have never failed me, told me that I wouldn't want him to get involved with any shenanigans or craziness, if there was going to be any.

When I arrived, there were two cop cars waiting outside.

"Ms. Amin?" one officer asked.

I was tired of hearing that question from an officer. So filled with solemnity, so filled with despair. Maybe it's me projecting, but I was so fucking tired of hearing that question.

"Yes," I said.

"We know you're here to pick Jaeda up," he said. "We talked to your daughter, and we know she doesn't want to go home with you. We're sorry."

"I understand, but I have a court order," I said, pulling the paper out of my purse, "that says I can take her with me."

"Well, you know, we can't allow you to do that. She said she doesn't want to go with you."

"Then what's the point of the court order?" I asked. "As far as I know, there has to be a valid reason. It can't be she just simply doesn't want to."

"Ma'am, we understand you're upset."

"It's Mother's Day," I said, feeling broken and worn down, with nothing left to offer but begging and reason.

"We can't force her to go with you," he said.

"You can help her disobey a court order, and you can prevent me from executing one?"

"We're sorry, but you'll need to go back to court if you want her to go with you."

"Mhmm, right," I said. "So you want me to go get another court order to tell you to help me execute this court order? And when I get that court order and you ignore it, are you going to tell me I need another one?!"

"Ma'am, we can't get involved in this," he said.

It's hard to explain the emotions I felt in that moment. If I had to begin, I would say that it was a mix of pure rage toward the situation, extreme sorrow for the loss of my daughter, and sheer confusion over everything else. All I wanted was my daughter back. All I wanted was to celebrate Mother's Day with my daughter. Was I asking for too much? Was there something I wasn't quite understanding? Had I behaved poorly? Nothing made sense anymore, and all I wanted to do was be with my children. Little did I know that the last time I picked her up would be the last time I would get to truly spend time with my daughter.

———◆———

I'd tried going to the police station before and gotten the same answer—that they didn't get involved in domestic situations like this. That there was no way they could force a child to get into a vehicle. They said that if the child was old enough to walk, talk, and understand, then that was a problem that the parents needed to handle. They said that if the child was a baby and in a car seat, maybe two or three years old, then they would understand. But when they couldn't physically move them, then the parents bore the onus, meaning they had to go back to the court system. But then I must ask, What's the point of a court order?

The entire situation, if you ask me, could have been avoided if court orders were actually enforced. My court order clearly stated that Jaeda and Aden were in my custody every other week. In a traditional marriage, if a child leaves the custody of the parent without permission, the police will help get that child back. For example, if a child runs away from home, they can't simply wander the streets, so the police will bring them home or to jail. So this begs the question—Why is it different just because the parents are divorced? Not enforcing the court order opens the door to parental alienation and manipulation. If the parents are not divorced, the argument that the child has a say in where they get to live is, to my knowledge, never valid and always ignored. If the parents are divorced, suddenly that argument has value.

I spent the rest of that night crying in secret. I didn't want Aden to be weighed down by this, so I would sneak off to my room and cry. I thought I was clever but apparently I was not, because Aden found me on the edge of my bed late in the evening.

"Hi, honey," I said, pushing the tissues off the other end of the bed and pretending as if I hadn't been crying. He sat down next to me and held my hand.

"Crying isn't going to bring Jaeda back," he said. My lip quivered, and I tried more than I have ever before to not cry. "You'll always have me, Mom. I'm here. I'll never leave you."

The dam of my tear ducts broke, and I sobbed. Not because I wanted Jaeda back—although I did—but because my son, the product of me, was right. I was so proud of him for being so wise, so proud of him for being his authentic self. They were tears of love. And my heart hurt.

———————

To understand my battle to get my kids back, you must understand the predicaments set forth by the United States legal system. You see, because of the way the United States of America was established—with big government having as little involvement with its people as possible—fighting for custody in court is a prickly endeavor and a burden that, although it can be relieved by lawyers immensely, truly falls on the parents. Maybe this is a good thing, but in my case, it wasn't, given the fact that I wasn't allowed to earn an income or a degree that would allow me to earn enough income to take care of my children until after I was divorced and fending for myself.

In October 2008 I was notified that we had a new court hearing. What could this possibly be about? I thought. During the hearing, Adder announced that his income had dropped to, if I remember correctly, $150,000 per year. Wait a minute, I thought, how could it have possibly dropped? He was still in the same job, still living in a multimillion-dollar home, still going on trips that were required in order to qualify for his title, and still owned four expensive cars. Not to mention the fact that our kids still went to a private school that cost $15,000 per year . He could afford all of that, yet he claimed his income had fallen below $150,000 per year?

Let me remind you, he was making $600,000 per year when I first filed for divorce. At that time, in 2008, I started receiving $11,000 per month in support. After that hearing in October 2008, I received approximately $5,700 per month. And by December of 2008, after another hearing, I received $2,069 per month due to his claim of lost income—yet still, he experienced no change in standard of living, all while the percentage of custody was radically changing.

It made no sense to me, but the courts don't care about that sort of thing. There is no one to investigate, so they believe what you say. The writing was on the wall, on his very, very fancy house's wall. And because of it, his alimony and child support payments dropped and I had to handle the burden.

There I was, a single mother trying to make it through school to get a well-paying job, and then this happened.

Not too long after, he took me back to court to fight for an even greater share of custody. At first we had 80-20 custody—80 percent for me and 20 for him. We had visited a minor's counsel lawyer, as directed by the court, and suddenly the kids announced that they wanted to spend more time with their father—something they never expressed to me. If they wanted that and had said it sooner, I of course would have let them. As horribly as he treated me, he was a decent father to them. So why deny them that? The judge decided that 50-50 custody was fair, and I agreed.

Just because Jaeda did not want to see me did not mean I wasn't still her mother. And it certainly didn't mean I wouldn't hurt. On her thirteenth birthday, I went to her school because they were enrolled in summer camp. I had a feeling she wasn't going to be receptive to my gifts and it was hot that summer, so I took her a cupcake, a Starbucks Frappuccino, and a Starbucks gift card. Normally for the kids' birthdays, I planned something fun for all of us to do together. For Aden's birthday that year, I took us ATV riding. This year was different, and so were we. Jaeda accepted the gift and said thank you. I was ecstatic!

The next day, when I saw Aden, he brought the gift card I had given Jaeda and said that she didn't want it.

"Wait, what? Then why did she thank me?" I asked.

"I don't know," he said.

I didn't want to bring Aden into the middle of it, so I accepted the card and ran the interaction over and over again in my head. I was noticing a pattern, and it hurt like hell. I knew that if the rejection had come from her directly, she would have done it in that moment, but because she wasn't the one who gave the card back to me, I had a feeling it was a decision coming from Adder. He had a history of rejecting gifts, and why would she reject the gift after she had accepted it? It all seemed too familiar, a pattern I couldn't ignore.

<hr />

All of the stress from this ongoing battle was starting to take a toll on me. Seemingly out of nowhere, I gained twenty or thirty pounds. My body wasn't used to such a sudden flux of weight, and it was scaring me.

When my work announced that we were attending an awards trip in Nashville, Tennessee, I thought that was just the vacation I needed—a little something to get my mind off of the tragic situation that my life had become. Even though a vacation could never cure what my family and I were going through, it was something to calm the nerves and bring me back to some semblance of a baseline.

My coworkers and I all went to the country bars—in the spirit of Nashville—and we even had Sheryl Crow perform for us at our awards dinner.

Then, seemingly out of nowhere, while in my hotel room one night, my heart rate picked up. A few months prior, I had experienced a quickened heart rate but it had only lasted a few minutes, so I sat down to wait it out. My chest hurt and it was horrifying, but it would just be another minute, I assured myself.

But then a minute turned into two, and then two more, and then two more.

Here I was in another state with no car and no clue what to do. It may have been a stupid move, but I waited about ten hours just trying to convince myself it would be a few more minutes. After ten hours passed, I couldn't breathe anymore. I couldn't lie down, and I certainly couldn't sleep. I tried to sleep sitting up, but even that wasn't working. There was an invisible beast sitting on my chest, and it hurt like hell. In the morning I called my mother for advice.

"What are you doing calling me?" she said with a raised tone. "Get to a hospital—now!"

Suddenly, my life started flashing before me. What if I die? I thought. What if this is how my life ends, while my relationship with my children is past the brink? All I wanted to do was to tell them I loved them.

I got on the hotel's shuttle and went straight to urgent care. The shuttle dropped me off at the bottom of the hill so I had no choice but to slowly walk up the hill to the urgent care.

"Ms. Amin, did you walk here?" the doctor asked as he was attempting to take my blood pressure.

"Yeah, it was the only way. Yeah, up the hill, just a couple blocks," I said.

"How long has this been going on?"

"About ten hours," I said, causing the doctor's jaw to drop, which is never a promising sign when you're in a doctor's office.

He removed the blood pressure machine and told me that because my heart was beating so fast, they couldn't get an accurate read. When they finally did, my heart rate was at 210 beats per minute.

"What I can tell you is that you must have a strong heart, Ms. Amin; otherwise you would have died of cardiac arrest many hours ago."

I tried to comprehend his words, but they only sunk in to the extent that I feared for my children. I knew they weren't a fan of me at that moment—to say the least—but if I were to pass away, who would be their mother? Who would help them to understand when Adder was misbehaving, as he frequently did? I couldn't leave my kids alone. Not this time.

"Ms. Amin?"

"Yes."

"You're not leaving here. You're going straight to the hospital in an ambulance. I'll have the nurse call one immediately."

In the ambulance they gave me a shot that essentially restarts your heart, as if it were a cell phone you could just reboot. I flatlined for a few seconds, and then my heart started beating again. All I remember was a feeling as if I was fading, similar to when you're on the cusp of sleep, and then a floating feeling, and then I was back. After my heart started beating at a normal pace, the ambulance rushed me to the hospital.

The only reason the doctors gave me for the experience was that it was instigated by stress.

I started to cry.

"I miss my kids," I said with my ugly crying face.

The doctor gave me one of those pouty sympathy faces, as if to say, "I am so sorry."

I missed my kids.

CHAPTER 8

Fool Me Once

*Then you will know the truth, and
the truth shall set you free.*
—John 8:32

I never wanted to be a boring mom. When I dreamed of having kids when I was younger, I knew that I didn't want to be like my parents in the sense that I wanted to be active with my kids. Not to say that my parents were bad in any sense of the word—far from it—but I wanted it to be different. If asked, I probably couldn't even give you an accurate count of the different activities we've done together, but the movies we've seen—oh, that's a different story. Going to the movie theater was one of our favorite pastimes.

After Jaeda left and the party was downgraded to two, I started buying more popcorn and candy, just to sweeten the deal for Aden even more. Or maybe it was to make him even happier so he knew how much I loved him. I don't really know. But no matter how much fun we had, there always came a moment during the movie in which all I could think about was the empty seat next to us. Each time I thought that

Jaeda's absence was a missed moment of bonding, I ate a piece of popcorn to ground my senses in reality and to help me forget about the pain. I told myself that maybe she wouldn't even remember moments like these because she was so young and that it was her older years that were truly important. Maybe this was psychosis, or maybe it was helpful. Either way, the pain still set in, and I did everything I could to make it go away. I looked forward to spending as much time as possible with her when she got older, to being there for her when she had kids and started a family. I wanted to be in on that action, and I prayed to God that we would be reunited by then. These are the thoughts that keep me going.

In Jaeda's absence, Aden and I got to spend even more time together one-on-one.

In Irvine they have a foam glow run where the track was set up with machines spraying soapy foam as you pass through. It was a little cold the day we went, but they had a dance party, which helped to keep us a little warmer. I went to take a video of Aden because he was dancing so much and having so much fun—a memory I wanted to remember forever—but when he saw the camera pointed at him, he abruptly stopped and turned away. That's odd, I thought. He's usually so performative when he sees a camera. Maybe he's embarrassed. But when a shadow lurks over your life, sometimes shadow thoughts sneak in as well. Or maybe, I thought, it was because he didn't want to be seen having fun with me?

A few weeks later, we went to Universal Studios Halloween Horror Night with Valerie's daughter, Annalise. Aden was a massive fan of horror and anything scary, and my mouth hurt by the end of the night from smiling at how much he loved it. Plus, it was the only way to mask the pain of not having Jaeda there. Our bond had become so strong, and in the absence of loss, the stronger bond soothed like honey.

One of the parts of my day I looked forward to most was picking Aden up from school. Not only because I could spend more time with him that way but also because I had hope that I would see Jaeda.

At a stoplight one day on the way to pick him up from school, I found a text from Aden.

"Mom, where are you?"

"I'm on the way. I'll be there in a few minutes," I responded.

"Ok."

Then, a few minutes later, he texted, "Mom, hurry up. Where r u?"

"I'm on my way. I'm right around the corner."

I pulled up next to him on the sidewalk and unlocked the door. I pulled down the visor to check my hair as I waited for him to get in. I closed the visor when I was done, but the door hadn't opened, so I looked over to see him still standing there. He's so silly, I thought. I rolled the window down.

"What are you doing?" I giggled.

He just stood there, his face stoic.

"Aden, what are you doing?" I said, losing the giggle. "Get in the car."

"I think I'm going to live with Dad," he said.

I remember hearing the words but not being able to process what he said. Was this really happening?

"Aden, stop. That's not funny. Get in the car."

"No."

"What do you mean 'No'? Get in the car."

"I'm not getting in the car," he said, firmer this time.

I pulled the car off to the side in complete shock. There was no way this was happening to me again. I had already lost one kid; I refused to lose two.

In my shock, the only productive thing I could think to do was to call my best friend for some levelheaded advice.

"I can't believe this is happening," I said. "It's happening again."

"What's happening again, friend?"

And that's when the nervous breakdown set in and she said she was on her way.

It's hard to describe the complete and utter pain a parent feels when she needs to rescue her child who doesn't want to be rescued but can only sob in a nervous breakdown instead. It's somewhere between feeling like a useless and a terrible parent. It leaves you questioning every move you've ever made, your own sanity, and the world around you. It leaves you yearning to wake up from the nightmare, knowing full well that you never will because this is real life.

Within the next twenty minutes, the principal arrived at the front of the school, as did Valerie. The principal asked if he could take Aden aside and talk with him as Valerie consoled me.

"Did you tell your mom this morning that you didn't want to go home with her?" the principal asked Aden.

"No."

"Well, you know, you can't really spring this on her without a conversation about it. Do you understand how this might be making her feel?"

"Yes," Aden said quietly.

"Is that fair? Your mom is here to spend time with you and pick you up. She is here to spend time with you, and you don't want to go, even though she legally has to pick you up."

Aden paused. "I still don't want to go with her."

Eventually the principal convinced Aden to come home with me.

Aden got in the car, threw his stuff on the floor, slammed the door, and said, "Are you happy now? I'm here. Are you happy you forced me to come and spend time with you? You got what you wanted."

In Aden's entire life, he had never spoken to me that way. This wasn't my child.

"What is wrong, Aden? Why are you acting like this?"

"I don't want to talk to you."

"Why? What did I do?"

"I don't want to be here is what's wrong. I want to be with Dad."

The only way I can describe the situation is it was like an alien movie, when the alien possesses the body of a human. They're still the same person physically, but their demeanor, their attitude, everything is different; they're a stranger. And Aden was my new stranger. We drove home in silence.

What if he asks to live with his dad again? I wondered on the drive home. What will I say if he asks? By the time I pulled into the driveway, I had decided that my answer would be no. I had learned my lesson the last time. I had allowed Jaeda to leave even though she said she'd return. I couldn't let that happen again.

The next day, as I took Aden to school, I had a gut feeling that if I dropped him off, something bad would happen. So then what? I thought. You don't drop him off ever again? You keep him locked in your house, protecting him from the outside world? The only alternative to dropping him off—which was keeping him home—was absolutely ridiculous and unrealistic, not to mention possessive, psychotic, and selfish. I could say it was to protect him, but was it? Either way, that's what mothers are supposed to do, right? Protect their kids? After hours of going back and forth with my options, I decided to drop him off.

All morning that gut-wrenching feeling persisted, so I swung past the school on his lunch break, and sure enough, the cops were there. The number of times I have said, "What the fuck?" to myself during my lifetime is definitely too many to count.

"I understand this is hard," the police officer said to me after she explained that Aden had called.

"No," I said. I was sick of people telling me they understood. They didn't understand. My mind was racing with rage and sorrow—an infuriating cocktail. I was at my breaking point, and I was questioning my own sanity too often at this point. There was no way the reality I perceived was real. It couldn't have been. The only rational explanation at that point was that I had lost my mind.

"No," I repeated. "You don't understand. You people keep telling me you understand, but you don't fucking understand. If you understood, then you wouldn't be here right now. If you all understood, I wouldn't be here right now. If you people understood even a fucking morsel of what was going on, I wouldn't be standing here questioning my own sanity right now."

It was at that moment that I became conscious of how loud I was talking, of how my body was shaking, and of how

concerned the officer looked. Suddenly I became overstimu-
lated and I was beyond aware of reality.

"Then help me understand," the officer said.

I launched into the spiel that I had nearly memorized since
I kept finding myself in this situation. And for the first time,
an officer, who happened to be a female, actually listened to
me. I cried. No one in the government had ever just listened,
let alone helped.

"I'll do my best to encourage him to go home with you,"
she said, "but you have to understand that I cannot force him.
I would not be legally allowed to do that, even if I wanted to."

And it worked. But just like the last time, I brought home
a stranger.

"Just because I'm going to live with dad doesn't mean I'm
not going to see you, Mom."

"Aden, that's exactly what your sister said to me." He
didn't say anything. "That's how your father is. If you think
you're going to have the ability to come back and see me,
you're wrong. Your father doesn't want that."

"Dad said if I wanted to, I could come back. So that's what
I'll do."

Later in the evening, I tried to talk to him about why exactly he didn't want to live with me anymore. Well, he explained, he wanted to spend more time with his sister.

"You mean your sister who, just two days prior, you said
was mean to you and whom you didn't want to go support at
the homecoming game?" I wasn't buying that excuse.

"Mom, I don't want to live with you."

I was getting nowhere. Even if—and I mean this—even
if I wasn't trying to convince him to stay with me—which I
was—at the minimum, I wanted to know why he didn't want

to live with me. It didn't make sense to me, despite the fact I had my suspicions. And it was becoming clear that the few excuses I was getting from him weren't true in the slightest.

—•—

The times between Aden's visits were few and far, so when he would ask to visit—which happened only twice—I was thrilled, if not a little thrown off. Jaeda never asked to come back and visit. I took him to see my parents to visit them and so he could get Christmas presents. We made cupcakes together and laughed with my mom and dad. The visit was short—a mere three hours—but those hours were precious. Three hours? I thought that sounded an awful lot like history repeating itself. That was the exact amount of time I was allowed with my parents when Adder gave me permission to go. When we got in the car to leave, during the second visit in March, I felt a chill run down my spine.

"Mom, can we go to my room?" Aden asked. "I want to see my room."

"Why do you want to see your room?" I asked.

"I just want to, OK?"

"Well, we don't really have time. If I had known, we could have left Grandma and Grandpa's house early, but we don't have time anymore. Unless you can ask your dad for more time?"

"No, I just wanted to see my room. It's OK."

"Are you sure? I can ask if you want."

"No, no. It's all right. It's OK. I don't feel good anyway."

"You don't feel good?"

"No. I just want to go home."

"Well, what did you want to go back home to do, anyway?"
He didn't reply.

"I just don't feel good anymore," he said.

"OK."

A few minutes passed, and then I asked, "When are you going to come back to see me?"

"Soon," he said.

"Do you promise?" I asked, trying to conceal my eagerness but clearly failing.

"I promise."

Aden reached over and held my hand—fingers interlaced, not just in each other's palms—something he hadn't done in I couldn't remember how long. He held my hand—and I his—for the rest of the car ride. We held them tight. I glanced over at him, and he smiled at me. And there, for a brief moment, time was suspended and all our problems were gone. There was no Adder. There was no craziness and abandonment. It was just us—mother and son, the love of my life.

When we approached his father's house, he quickly dropped my hand. I put the car in park and leaned over to hug him. He gave me a quick hug, picked up his bag, then hopped out, saying, "Bye, Mom, love you," and dashed for the front door. And just like that, our moment was gone.

"I love you too," I said as soon as I could but after the door shut. I love you too.

Over the next few days, I texted him and asked when he was coming back to see me but didn't get a firm answer. Those days turned into weeks, and those weeks—as I bet can be inferred—turned into months. I texted as much as I could without being overbearing while still being his mother. All I could do was remember our last moments together, that car ride fueled with so much love. Every time I sent a text, I wondered why on earth he wanted to go see his room. And the more texts I sent, the more it seemed that he knew that was going to be the last time I saw him. And as much as I held out hope, I was beginning to run on empty.

CHAPTER 9

The Fight of My Life

Once the storm is over, you won't remember how you made it through, how you managed to survive. You won't even be sure, in fact, whether the storm is really over. But one thing is certain. When you come out of the storm, you won't be the same person who walked in.
—Haruki Murakami

It was starting to seem as if nobody in the court system had my back. Slowly, yet more and more, it seemed as if I was losing my children, despite loving them more and more each day. So after Jaeda left, I began documenting everything. I saved every movie ticket, every piece of paper I received from the courts; every time the kids were with me, I wrote down when I picked them up and when I dropped them off at their father's. And the only reason I did this was it was the only way I could think of to fight fairly for my children.

I attended just about every baseball, volleyball, and softball game the kids had. And at every game the kids had, I was treated like a stranger. There are two sides to every story, but no one ever tells you that the other side—no matter which side—is lying. In the sphere of parental alienation, with no legal system to investigate, you can never be certain about which side is telling the truth and which side is not. Back when I was with David, we noticed the kids' behavior changing. I went to see a therapist since I couldn't get Adder to consent to taking the kids. I went, described what was happening, and requested her input and recommendations regarding integrating our families and the comments the kids were making.

She said that based on what I had told her, it sounded like a classic case of parental alienation.

"Parental what?" I asked, having never heard the term before.

"Parental alienation," she clarified. "That's when one parent essentially manipulates the couple's children into believing the other parent is not a good parent. Eventually, the children can become alienated from the supposed 'bad parent,' even if that parent is actually the good parent."

I was shocked; she had just described my situation.

Parental alienation was first termed in the 1980s by Dr. Richard A. Gardner. He described it just as my therapist did, adding that the alienating parent often lodges false accusations at the other parent. They try to keep the children away from the other parent, which gives them a better chance of instilling lies in the child's head. And when the other parent isn't there to prove the lies wrong, to defend themselves, the lies—especially in the minds of young children—can become truths. On January 15, 2015 The Association for Psychological Science wrote "Memories are so easily manipulated that in 3 hours you can be convinced you committed a crime that never happened. Researchers did a study in order to understand more about why people have gone to jail for false confessions, and they were able to convince 70% of participants that they were guilty of a fake crime. The participants not only confessed, they described very detailed experiences that never actually happened". What's more, this parent, Gardner explained, can often afford to take the other party to court. When I first learned all of this, all I could think was did someone teach this to Adder before he even met me decades ago? It all felt too real, and I wanted it to be over. I wanted to have my children back in my arms. I wanted to forget everything that happened with my parents, to love them like I did before we ever met Adder. But there we were, so I had to own it, to grow from it.

What's more, according to a survey conducted by the Association of Family and Conciliation Courts in 2014, there is a 98 percent agreement "in support of the basic tenet of parental alienation that children can be manipulated by one parent to reject the other parent who does not deserve to be rejected." If my children and I weren't already walking proof of parental alienation, here was the statistic to back it up.

As a mother, you want to knock down the offending parent's front door, take your kids under your wing, and run. You want to tell them that the lies they've been fed are just that— lies. You want to be their mother. You want to protect them. A mother's instinct is primal, primitive. It borders rage yet is balanced by and rooted so deeply in love that it could never be rage. I wanted nothing more than to take my kids and run. *The law said I couldn't.* And even if I could knock down his front door and take my babies back home, they, at the time, probably wouldn't even have wanted to come because they'd been led to believe that I was a terrible mother, that I didn't care about them. So there I was, left totally and utterly helpless, rendered a bad mother by falsities, and in the eyes of the courts, just another side of the story.

In 1977 George L. Engel created the biopsychosocial model. In short, this model exhibits the connection between biology, psychology, and socioenvironmental factors. In the case of parental alienation, the biopsychosocial model examines the effects the alienation has on both the parents and the children in terms of their health (both physical and mental) and the conscious and subconscious mind. In other words, the model examines, based on the effects of alienation, how an individual evolves in the wake of such alienation.

Take, for example, my situation. On the multiple occasions Child Protective Services was called on me for abuse, my children were effectively told, subconsciously, that I had abused them when no abuse actually occurred. What kind of message did that send to my children? How will that lie affect them as they grow up? The possibilities are endless, but the most realistic and likely outcome is severe trust issues, especially when it comes to authority.

The scary part of parental alienation is the blatant disregard for the child's well-being. The alienating parent, often to some degree a narcissist, uses the child as a weapon, doing what they must to take predominate custody of the child. And in the process, a good parent can be taken from the child. The child's best interest is thrown to the wayside, and at what cost? So the alienating parent can win!

Even scarier is that some experts believe that the accusations the alienating parent lodges are projections of his or her own behavior. For example, the father who complains that the mother is verbally abusive may just be the verbally abusive parent himself. Some experts say that this is a borderline disorder, which isn't uncommon in parental alienation situations. For example, the alienating parent may resort to a tactic called splitting, which is when they will recruit other individuals—not just the children but also family members and friends—to be supporters and essentially fight alongside them.

In my case, Adder's mother, sister, and brother were all recruited to keep my own children away from me. Anytime I happened to run into my kids in public, they were quickly escorted back to the car or directed in the opposite direction by one of the recruits, as I called them. God forbid I get to see or talk to my kids, the humans I gave birth to and raised. The humans I loved so much. The humans I loved more than anything in this world. All I wanted was to love my kids.

Although I'm not one to harp on the past, I have never been able to figure out what the point of all of this was. Why me? Why my children? My entire relationship with Adder felt plotted and planned. But the fact of the matter is—as I discovered years later—parents who engage in alienating behavior usually do so because they themselves are unhealthy. While Adder was incapable of having a normal, trusting, and loving relationship with me, I was incapable of being the typical Syrian woman for him. I wasn't interested in submitting and living a life of nothing. And he was only interested in controlling me. Thus, when I divorced him, it became his mission, whether he realized it or not, to destroy my relationship with my children. So now, I suppose, the question becomes, Why my children? Why couldn't he just leave them out of it?

There are a few signs that you can look out for if you suspect any degree of parental alienation.

The child may simply refuse to talk to or visit you, assuming everything said by the alienator parent is correct. Or they may give a not-so-convincing reason for not meeting you. This is referred to as frivolous rationalization. And it has been the situation since the day my kids left. The excuse their dad always uses to address the court and authorities is "The kids say they don't want to."

The child is not allowed to or "chooses" not to contact any other family members related to the alienated parent. Since May 8, 2015, Jaeda has not had contact with any of my family members. And since March 12, 2017, Aden has not had any contact with any one of my family members.

The child may be rude and show hatred toward you and your extended family or friends. Multiple times I would receive bizarre text messages from the children in which they said rude things. I am convinced it was not them speaking but rather a message from someone else.

The child may have no feelings of guilt for their wrong behavior. Now this is bone-chilling. To look into your children's eyes and see nothing but cold, dead eyes staring back at you, almost as if they are not even looking at you, is horrifying, but it's a warning sign.

The child may talk wrongly about you in front of others, such as teachers or friends. This is referred to as spreading animosity.

The child may perceive everything coming from the alienator parent as "good" or "right" and everything related to you as "bad" and "wrong." This indicates a lack of ambivalence , having no emotional connection to the targeted parent, in the child. Simple example, one day I was helping the kids with their math homework and anything I said to them was instantly rejected and followed by, "This isn't how dad does it. His way is better."

The child may not accept anything positive coming from you. And they may always take the side of the alienator parent. This is referred to as reflexive support. Which essentially is the alienating parent plants in the child's mind that they are the victim so the child feels the need to come to their rescue.

The child may not be able to gauge what is right and wrong but believes whatever the alienator parent says.

The first child is made responsible for the other children by the alienator. They are treated by the alienator as very entitled, and this makes them feel like they have the power. They are also put in a position in which they believe they have to take care of the alienating parent.

A perfect example of this: I picked up the kids from school one day, and went to basketball practice, then started to head home. Suddenly, Jaeda yelled out, "Oh my God! We have to go back to the school."

"Why?" I asked. "What's wrong?"

She said that she forgot to get a book for Aden that her dad put her in charge of. I asked Aden if he needed it to complete his homework, and he said no. So I told Jaeda he could get it tomorrow, that it was no big deal. She started crying, shaking, and begging me to get it and said she would be in big trouble if she didn't. I told her that she didn't have to worry about it because it was not her responsibility, that Aden was old enough to learn to be responsible for his own belongings. She wouldn't stop crying until I went back to the school and got the book. One would wonder why Adder didn't just give the book to Aden. Both kids were with him. Why put that stress and responsibility on Jaeda when he could have easily put it in Aden's backpack?

I was able to finally get a court order to have a few therapy sessions with the children. The therapist met with me and their dad together. She also met with me and the children in a joined session and the children with their father in their own session. After the required sessions were over, the therapist met with me to discuss her findings. She specifically said to me "it is clear that their father would rather walk on broken glass than be in the same room with you. It is also clear that he is grooming the children". I left her office feeling empowered and hopeful that this can help me in court! When we went back to court to try and enforce visitation with my kids, the therapist tells the court "mom needs to back off". What?! How in the world can she tell me that he is grooming the children then completely change her opinion in court? All I can say about that is money talks. Feel free to make your own conclusion as to how her opinion changed.

Some courts may use a parental alienation checklist to identify the behavior of a child and to relate it to parental alienation. The standard checklist includes:

- Bad-mouthing the other parent
- Lying to the child by saying that the other parent doesn't love them anymore
- Expressing anger or withdrawing love to pull the child away from the other parent
- Making the child dependent and creating a distance between them and the alienated parent
- Limiting contact between the child with the alienated parent

- Pressuring or forcing the child to pick one of the two parents
- Brainwashing the child that the other parent could be dangerous
- Not allowing the other parent to visit the child
- Making the child check on or spy on the parent
- Changing the child's name so that there's no association with the other parent
- Hiding information about the child from the alienated parent
- Telling the child not to call the other parent Mom or Dad and instead asking them to call the parent by their first name
- Creating fear in the child about court, trial, and litigation procedures
- Interfering in the child and parent's communication
- Limiting pictures of the child with the other parent

This checklist can be used by the attorneys and the judge to understand the situation and also the proof as presented by the alienated parent. This list was definitely not used in my case. Any and all evidence I showed to prove parental alienation was dismissed.

Judges are given so much power in the American family court system. Basically, they are required to rule "in the best interest of the children," which, quite frankly, is a very broad statement that is open for interpretation. There are no guidelines as to what would be considered "in the best interest of the children." Every judge decides what that means. It is hard to accept that a loving mother who is highly educated, career-driven, has no addictions, shows up to almost all school and sporting events, volunteers at the school regularly, and has a squeaky-clean record would not be considered "in the best interest of the children."

The family court legal system needs to change! A child who has no legal authority to make any other major decisions in their life should not be allowed to choose to eliminate a parent from their life, as long as there is no evidence of abuse and or negligence, of course. Even then, there should be some contact, such as supervised visitation and phone calls, all of which I did not get. Parents have a constitutional right to direct the care, upbringing, and education of their children. This is under the Due Process Clause of the Fourteenth Amendment. All of that was taken from me with no cause. How can a judge allow a twelve-year-old to make a choice as to "the best interest of the child"? The long-term repercussions of a child not having a mother or father in their life are devastating both emotionally and psychologically.

Once that "choice" is taken off the table, it eliminates the power of the alienator; if the child is legally obligated to comply with the court-ordered custody agreement, then the emotional and psychological control that the alienator has will disappear. That pressure will be lifted off the child.

Let's look at this from a financial standpoint. If a parent is deprived of a relationship and any contact with their children, they should not be forced to pay child support. I bet if having a relationship and regular contact was a precondition of collecting child support, the alienator would miraculously allow contact. I have been paying child support for years and at the same time, have been deprived of a hug, a kiss, even a phone conversation with my children. The alienator is being allowed to emotionally and psychologically damage the children and the alienated parent while getting paid to do it!

What's worse is that the judge has the power to literally turn your children's lives upside down and never has to answer for it. Why? Because judges have immunity. Any other person who puts you through that kind of emotional distress would have their day in court and pay for what they put you through. Sadly, not in this case.

A friend once asked me if I would ever be able to move on from this tragedy, if there would ever be a time at which I could go back to normal. How could I? It still feels as if I have lost my children—these beautiful humans whom I gave birth to, whom I raised, in whom I instilled values. I am aware that I will need to do a lot of work on myself to be able to live a normal life without my children.

Although I have hope that someday they'll return, the pain and sense of loss are still the same. Holidays are full of grief, and birthdays are unbearable. If this is the tragedy that I experience, I can't imagine what it must be like for my children. Although they may dislike—God forbid hate—me now, deep down I have hope that they still love me. But in that same breath, if that is true and they do still love me, then they, too, must be experiencing a feeling of bereavement, and I pray every day that they do not. I just want them to be happy. But even if they do not love me, they still have to cope with the loss of a parent, no matter how much they may dislike me. They have witnessed the devastating effects of my separation from Adder. It's a silent form of abuse, and I can't even protect my children from it.

And as for me, God how I wish I could protect myself from it. I wish I didn't have to plead to the authorities powerlessly to help get my children back. And how I wish I could just get over it, go back to a time in which I could "go back to normal," as my friend said. It's just not that simple. Grief is never that simple. And unfortunately, grief isn't that short either.

If one understands life through the Kübler-Ross grief model, then one can only assume that it would take just as long for an alienated parent to grieve the alienation of their child as it would the passing of a child. Now, I'm not comparing the death of one's child to the alienation of a child from a parent, but they are similar. The difference is that with alienation, there is still hope that the child will return home. The thing about hope, though—the thing they don't tell you—is that it can be an incessant little thing that can eventually wear you down. As lovely as it is to have hope, over time too much hope can drive you insane; it can rip at you and turn you into a beggar. So you do your best and hope that you can navigate the stages of grief as perfectly as possible.

It starts with shock and denial. You start to see the signs. You notice that your child is talking differently and acting more neutral around you or maybe even cold toward you. You will be shocked by this behavior because, well, your child would never behave this way. It's almost as if they have a bad influence. And when it gets worse, when your child becomes distanced and you reach out to the authorities with no help in return, you deny reality.

Although the shock never really passes, you eventually move on to the next stage of grief, which is an emotional volcano. And because the shock never really passes, it leaves you questioning just about everything, which never really stops. Although my children have yet to come home, I hope that the confusion and inquisition stop when they return. But in the meantime, the emotions take over. Sometimes it will take the form of walking past your child's room and shedding a tear. Sometimes you will sob uncontrollably when making their favorite meal for dinner. You know, that kind of heart-wrenching cry that brings you to your knees. Where you think that someone will have to pry you off the ground and force you to continue living. And God forbid anything atrocious happens as a result of the alienating parent's behavior. Say, for example, you deliver a present to your child's school on their birthday and they text you a picture later of that gift in the trash. The tears will come harder those days, and the rage toward the alienating parent will be much worse.

Which leads to the next stage—anger. Almost as if a result of the confusion—of asking yourself questions like, "How could this happen?" or "Why me?"—the anger will settle in quickly. You'll start to remember all the little microaggressions, all the lies, all the abusive behavior, whether silent or noticeable. You'll remember how the authorities didn't take action—or at least not as much action as you wanted them to. It's even possible for this anger to be cast upon the people who don't deserve it, people like your innocent family members or friends. You don't mean to be angry at them, but you also don't realize why you are. It's all misguided rage that should be directed toward the alienating parent.

I'm grateful that I am part of this generation, which acknowledges the correlation between our emotions and our physical health. As science has proven, worry and sorrow can quite literally suppress our immune systems and make us more susceptible to illness. Our bodies produce fewer lymphocytes and T-cells, which are the white blood cells that are crucial for fighting diseases. The pain you might experience as a result of your lost child can result in nausea, headaches, fatigue, and even diarrhea. Lack of sleep can elicit the same result.

Once this stage sets in, and usually only then, do you start to worry about yourself. It's almost an out-of-body experience, where you can see your body but you know it's not the real you. You know the way you're behaving isn't who you want to be. You start to worry and maybe even panic. You may even cast harsh judgment on yourself, ready to ignore the person you see and revert to a stage of denial.

And the next stage of the grief process is usually where guilt rears its head. You'll once again start to question your behavior, except this time, that concern is directed toward your past self. The plethora of what-ifs will hit you full force, and you'll wonder if there was something you could have done—anything, just anything—to change what happened. The fact of the matter is, though, there isn't and there never will be.

The depression will get worse as all of these stages pile on top of each other. Your relatives may start to grow distant because they just don't know how to support you. It's not their fault. But you will notice this, and you'll start to think of yourself as alone.

Of course, at a certain point, you must reenter society. You'll be forced to establish a routine. You'll notice the holes in your routine that your children once filled. You'll find yourself calling out to them from down the hallway only to be greeted by silence. You'll find yourself making a plan based on their schedule, only to remember that you have all the time in the world to yourself.

And it's because of this that hope—that beautiful, sometimes nefarious little thing—is important. Your instinct will be to cast this feeling aside. You'll ignore it and, quite frankly, do whatever you can to avoid it at all costs. But that is why you need it now more than ever. An easy way to go about retaining hope is to do what most alienated parents think is unbearable—accept. Accept that what happened has happened and that nothing about it will change. This is the toughest part of having children be alienated from you, but once you achieve it, life becomes just a little bit easier. This doesn't mean you should ignore your feelings or stop feeling sad, angry, or guilty. Rather, it means you should accept reality for what it is and use that as a source of energy to overcome, to preserve your sanity.

Holidays are never easy when the two people you love more than anything—including yourself—aren't there to celebrate with you. It's not just that; it's also knowing that they are off somewhere else—without you. But once some time passes, you learn to put on a mask and pretend like you're enjoying yourself completely, knowing deep down that part of your soul is missing.

Instead of sitting at home—time I would usually spend with the kids—I celebrated all the holidays at my parents' so I could be around my family. But there always came a time when I had to go home alone to an empty house where the ghosts of my past danced in the shadows. Those nights were the worst; they still are. The pain of not having my kids with me was too much, so I never bothered to decorate. Why? So I could be miserable in a cheerful place? When you're depressed, that's the last thing you want to do. If I had put up a tree, it would have felt as if I was celebrating without my kids, as if I was moving on—and I didn't want to move on. I wanted them with me.

When I got home from my parents', a deafening silence welcomed me. I wondered how long this would last and whether I would ever return to a normal state, to a state of happiness, to a state of love—a state that included my children.

CHAPTER 10

Keep Up the Good Fight

I will never stop writing my story in ink.
I need to leave my children proof that
pain can be transformed into beauty.
—Unknown

Two years passed before I was able to put up a tree again, before I realized that putting up a tree didn't mean I was moving on from my children. Putting up a tree didn't mean that I wasn't fighting to get my kids back in other ways. It didn't detract from me still being their mother. Rather, it allowed me to work on myself, to build myself up so I could continue to fight even harder. What would my kids do if they decided to come back home and found me beat-up, bruised, and torn down? No. I needed to be at my best for when they came back—whenever that would be.

I had to let that go and say to myself, Fine, just because my kids aren't here, that doesn't mean everything else dies. They say that time heals, but I don't believe it actually does.

It doesn't change anything. It doesn't bring back loved ones who have moved on. I can still cry at the drop of a dime if a memory of the kids is recalled. Rather, time simply makes it easier to bear the burden. It's sort of like when you're all cried out and the only thing left to do is accept the reality and the emotions and find a way forward. I was able to find that path forward—a path that allowed me to continue to fight for my kids while also putting myself first. I was able to come to terms with the fact that I was in a temporary period of sorrow and loss. I was able to come to terms with the fact that one day I would be reunited with my children but I would have to put in the work if I wanted that to happen.

If you are experiencing parental alienation, please know that there is a light on the other side. Please know that there are things you can do to move forward. They may not bring your child back to you, but they can make your life more bearable, they can make you stronger, and they can make life worth living again.

It's important to keep in mind that getting to a place where you are better (and getting your kids back) will take time. Unfortunately, there isn't one single action you can take to get your kids back quicker—at least not one I can legally recommend. So the first step you need to take is to surrender to the fact that you can certainly still fight for your kids but time needs to work its magic and surrender to the fact that you cannot control time. Once you do that, you create a healthier foundational mindset from which you can more successfully fight for your children.

Which leads to the next step: taking care of *you*. The metaphor is certainly overused in today's self-help market, but that's because it's true: just as on an airplane in the event of an accident, you must put your oxygen mask on first before you try to save others. If you are draining yourself of time, money, and energy, when your kids finally do return to you, you will be a shell of your former self, which means you won't be able to be fully present for your kids when they will need you most.

The best way to start "putting your oxygen mask on first" is to discover your purpose. If you don't have a purpose for which to live, getting out of bed in the morning will be tough, if not impossible. As you lay in bed, you'll think, Why? Why should I even bother? This bed is cozy, and the world outside is not. Having something to look forward to will allow you to counter this false narrative you have so cleverly (and unintentionally, mind you) crafted. And I know I sound like a broken record here, but keep in mind that having a purpose outside of your kids doesn't mean you aren't still fighting for them; it just means that you are taking care of *yourself.* When your kids return, you want them to see you as strong, as someone who didn't allow the horrible situation to break you, as someone who survived and thrived. I know that's what I want my kids to see when they come back.

If you struggle to shift your mindset, try this on for size. Instead of thinking, I am living because of my kids, think, When my kids return, I am a strong support system that they can rely upon. Your goal is still the same—to be the best support for your children—the only difference is the method you are using. And just imagine what your kids will think of you when they return home to see that you are a strong pillar of hope and love rather than a shell of a human. They *want* to see you succeeding and thriving.

I wish I had known this years ago. When Jaeda left, I was distraught. I didn't allow myself time to heal because I thought

Aden needed me. I still had another child to care for and love; how could I possibly worry about myself when my other child was in need? My purpose in the aftermath became taking care of Aden, and only taking care of Aden, since anything related to Jaeda was out of my control. Of course I was fighting for Jaeda, but on the home front, Aden was the priority. I allowed this false narrative to penetrate my mind, which caused further chaos down the road. When Aden left, suddenly I was left with no purpose. I had no one to take care of. I involuntarily became a mother without children. When I finally realized that I needed to shift my mindset and create a new purpose, I started smiling again. By that point, I was all cried out of tears. I was still in extreme sorrow, don't get me wrong; I still missed my kids more than anything and was fighting for them daily. But this time I was able to put my oxygen mask on first.

I would be remiss if I didn't mention the fact that in the beginning, when your children are first taken from you or leave you, you won't be thinking about how you can make the situation easier. You will most likely be simply surviving one day at a time. You will be flooded with emotions that you most likely won't know how to amend. You'll probably feel a lot of guilt, anger, and sorrow. The most important tool to remember in that moment is naming and validation. When you realize you are feeling an intense emotion, label it. Is it anger you're feeling? Is it sorrow? Is it frustration? What about disappointment or rejection? Whatever the emotion, make sure you put a name on it. The more specific you can get, the better.

Then, once you name it—and only after you name it, as if you skip naming, the following step will not work—make sure you validate that emotion. Something as simple as saying, "It is OK that I feel [insert emotion]" works great. Keep in mind that all emotions always, no matter what, are valid. We cannot help which emotions we feel. Ever. There is a distinct difference between a thought and an emotion. Make sure you are not validating thoughts—only emotions.

If you live with the constant bombardment of others' opinions or if you live in a culture that judges you if you aren't constantly fighting for your kids (rather than fighting for yourself so you can fight for your kids), then try your hardest to block that negative energy out. At the end of the day, you are the only person who knows what is best for you. Trust your gut. Make decisions that are in your best interest, not in the best interest of an outside opinion.

There will be times when you are worried about whether you are going to make the right decision. That's OK. Remind yourself that you are not responsible for making the *right* decision. Expecting yourself to make the right decision all the time is dangerous territory. It's unreasonable and, quite frankly, a little narcissistic. So don't worry about making the right decision; worry about making the *best* decision—the decision that is best for you and your children. See how it's all about shifting your mindset?

Every day, my inner gremlin pops up and makes me wonder if I made the right decisions in my story. Was it right to not let Jaeda come home with me all those months? Was it right to let Aden live with his father, despite me having partial custody? The honest answer to these questions, quite frankly, is I'm not sure. But what I am sure of is that at the time, I made the decision I thought was best; I let them know what the consequences would be and trusted them to make the best decision, and I stand by that to this day, despite not being sure if it was the *right* decision. I did my best, and that is enough to be proud of. I'm not a superhero. I'm not God. It is not my responsibility to be perfect.

If you struggle with remaining confident in your decisions, then write out a list of your morals and values. Take an hour to sit down in your happy place—that could be your desk, the beach, a coffeehouse, the bathtub, literally anywhere you feel happy—and think about what your values are. Do you value honesty? Integrity? Authenticity? Compassion? Love? Loyalty? Kindness? Self-respect? If you ever find yourself questioning your choices and decisions, refer back to your list of values. Did you violate your values by that choice? No? Then you have no reason to feel shame, guilt, fear, or any other negative emotion since you were behaving within your values. If you decide that you did violate your values by behaving a certain way, then forgive yourself. Make amends if your decision hurt someone else. And more importantly, decide how you will not behave that way again and then forgive yourself.

There may even be times where you realize that you didn't behave according to your values or you made a decision that wasn't in your or your children's best interest. These moments are tough because then the guilt becomes justified. The situation can be made worse if there are spectators. I won't lie, these moments suck, and everyone has them every once in a while. It's called being human. In these moments it's even more important to practice naming and validating and then forgiveness. Acknowledge the emotion—most likely guilt. Tack a name onto that emotion, figure out why it is you feel that emotion, and then surrender. Say to yourself, "Yeah, this happened. I don't agree with my decision in retrospect, but I now know why I do not agree." It takes so much courage to admit you didn't behave within your values or to admit that you think what you did wasn't up to your standards. In other words, it takes courage to admit that you were wrong. Finding the courage to admit it will make you even stronger.

Once you name and validate, don't forget to do something nice for yourself. Go for a walk, call a friend, get an ice cream, donate to a charity. It doesn't matter what you do; all that matters is that you do something that makes you feel good, something that makes you feel happy. Give yourself permission to move on from that situation.

Your inner gremlin might try to trick you into thinking that if you do this, if you let go of this guilt, then you will be dismissing the situation. I'm here to tell you that this is not true in the slightest. Do not associate guilt with forgetting. Just because you have forgiven yourself doesn't mean you didn't pay the price. It doesn't mean that you are not taking responsibility for what happened. Think of it this way: Let's say you're trying to reach that last box of cereal on the top shelf at the grocery store. They always say not to climb, but there's no one around, so you just can't help but climb. Halfway up the shelf, it tips over and lands on top of you. No one is around to help. You wouldn't just lie there feeling guilty, thinking, well, this is my fault, so I guess I'd better stay here. No, you would do whatever you had to in order to get that shelf off of you. It's called doing the work that is necessary. This doesn't mean that the situation never happened. You won't continue on lying to yourself by telling yourself that it never happened. Rather, you will remember what happened. You will acknowledge that it was a terrible situation, but then you will allow yourself to do the work to get out of that situation. You may think of it from time to time, but you have to give yourself permission to move on, to continue to fight—for your children's sake.

If you are religious or spiritual, you may even wonder what the bigger meaning is behind your children leaving or being taken away from you. You may wonder why the higher power in charge—whatever that is for you—is doing this to you and more importantly, why it is doing this to your kids. Why would it put a child in such a terrible situation? But let's be honest here—there very likely will never be an answer to these questions, so it's important not to fall into an existential spiral over this. You'll want to beg for an answer to these questions because you are the protector of your kids. You are the parent; therefore, you have assumed the role of doing whatever you have to in order to protect your children. You need to release the need to know the answer. To do that, start by acknowledging that this is not a need; it is a desire. Once again, you'll need to shift your mindset and way of thinking. Instead of thinking, Why is this happening to me? think, Why is this happening for me, and how can it make me stronger? The only thing you *need* to do in this world is take care of yourself and your children. Once you acknowledge that it is a desire and not a need, it will be easier to release the thought and accept that you may never know. Use this acceptance as fuel for hope.

Of course, it doesn't hurt to wonder, so I'm certainly not saying to never think about it. Rather, don't let the curiosity become unhealthy by way of obsession. Obsession is an unhealthy coping mechanism that is often unintentionally employed by the lizard brain (more scientifically referred to as the reptilian complex) because your brain thinks that is what is necessary in order for you to survive.

Find trust. I know, it's hard to find trust when life has backhanded you, but know that the universe is made of love. At the root of everything in this world is love. Trust that love will help you survive.

I've thought a lot about the greater meaning of my and my kids' struggle and eventually concluded that this may not even be about me. Perhaps this is happening because my children are being molded to be stronger than ever. Maybe it's happening because Adder needed to be taught a lesson. Who knows? Not me. And I'm OK with that. At the end of the day, I have only been made stronger and more resilient.

It wasn't until I attended a transformational program that I finally started to become better and healthier. Before I attended, I was at my lowest point. I thought nothing would help me get my kids back, and I thought the rest of my life would be sheer torture. I was ready to give up. My gremlin mind fed me all of these lies that kept me in bed an unhealthy amount of time. Fighting for my kids became my life and my obsession. A dear friend of mine, Destiny, worried about me and had previously attended this transformational program with great success. I didn't believe it would work, but I trusted her, and it changed my life. It helped me shift my mindset in radical ways—turning every negative, gremlin thought into a positive—helped me see the negative narratives I was telling myself, and helped me to realize that I could be as powerful as I wanted, that nothing could hold me back except for myself.

Because transformational programs can be so powerful and beneficial, I recommend starting one even if you're not in as serious a situation. If you're going through a divorce or even contemplating a separation, join a transformational program now! It will open your eyes to so many aspects of your thought process and subconscious mind, allowing you to better understand other people and their thought processes. It can teach you how to be understanding and empathetic rather than reactive and defensive. Essentially, it can teach you perspective.

———————

If you haven't already gathered it from this chapter, the most important advice I have for a parent who has been alienated from their children is to take care of yourself first. If you don't, you won't be able to be there for your kids when they return. Part of taking care of yourself is—and I apologize for the buzzword fever I'm about to unleash on you, but it's true—practicing self-care. Now, the term "self-care" has been thrown around a lot in the last decade, often in an unhealthy way. I want you to know that self-care isn't just meditation and eating kale. It's so much more than that. What people often seem to get wrong about self-care is they completely ignore the most important aspect—your *self*. In other words, practicing self-care means engaging in behaviors or activities that help you to tend to your emotional, physical, and spiritual self. If eating kale isn't your thing, then don't do it. If meditation isn't your thing, great news—you don't have to meditate.

Creating a self-care routine starts with discovering the activities that make you feel good, activities in which you genuinely enjoy engaging. You want to remind yourself who you are as a person. Remember, this isn't disregarding your children. You're not creating an image of yourself as a nonparent.

Rather, you're creating a vision of you that exists when your kids aren't around.

For me, this became travel. I so desperately wanted to get out of the bubble I had formed around myself. I wanted to be somewhere I wouldn't run into Adder or his recruits at the grocery store. I wanted to be somewhere that wasn't associated with my life. I wanted to create my own universe, and I knew I wouldn't run into family members or friends in Prague. I would go on trips across the world and trips in my own state of California—anywhere I could get away. More importantly, I went places that I hoped I could one day take my children to. If I had a suspicion my kids would like that place, I would scope it out first by vacationing there in hopes that one day I could take them. And every place I went, I bought them souvenirs that I will one day give them.

Some other ideas for self-care include going on a hike, getting a massage, taking yourself out to dinner, getting drinks with a friend, or even something as simple as calling a friend when you're feeling down. Discover your nighttime skincare routine. Take bubble baths with candles lit. Take an hour out of each day to read a book. Whatever makes you feel warm. More importantly, make sure that you don't fall into the trap of isolation. A lot of self-care techniques can be isolating, so if you find yourself spending too much time with yourself, reach out to a friend. When I first started healing, I promised myself that I would say yes to at least one event per week. This went on for a little while and allowed me to reenter society after I had isolated for far too long. Eventually, I moved the goal post to twice a week, and so on. This became so successful that I completely forgot about my rule at one point and was going out when I felt like it. That's the beauty of healing—if you sacrifice yourself to healing, to love, you won't even know it's happening.

Not too long after Aden left, I started having dreams about him and Jaeda. In the beginning they just made an appearance. I can't remember when, but at one point, the dreams became solely about my children. In a way, I think this was the universe's way of giving me time to spend with my children. I know that sounds crazy, but it's true. And every time I have a dream about them—which is nearly daily—I wake up happy because I was able to see my kids. There's a bond between mother and child, and my mind refuses to let that bond be broken despite the physical connection being absolved.

I'm by no means a dream expert, but what I do know is that nearly all dreams hold meaning. Not too long after Aden left and I was essentially living at home alone, unsure of when my kid would return, I had a vivid dream. I was outside of what seemed to be the kids' former preschool. It was a brick building, and the sky was the bluest I'd ever seen it. To the right of the school, Jaeda and Aden were standing under a jacaranda tree that was in full bloom with deep lilac and amethyst purple leaves. The kids were younger, and once they noticed me, they came running. They had backpacks on, as if they were coming from school. We embraced and cried together. It wasn't until I came up for air that I noticed Adder standing in the doorway of the school—staring at us. He didn't say anything and never moved; he just lurked and stared.

I woke up thrilled. I couldn't believe the kids had run to me given that they both had recently chosen to live with their father. This, I decided, was their way of visiting me and saying hi.

I needed to be close to them that day. I had this overwhelming need to see my children. So, I went to one of their favorite Middle Eastern restaurants, a place we used to go. If I couldn't be with them physically, I thought, I might as well honor them this way by eating their favorite flatbreads with delicious cheese and veggies. I sat facing the window so I could appreciate the beauty of the landscape. Within minutes of sitting down, I saw a car pull up with Keres's brother driving. Once the car was parked, Jaeda and Aden got out of the back and then Keres out of the passenger side. Did I manifest this? I wondered.

When they entered the building, Keres's brother noticed me and turned his back. Keres and her brother whispered to each other and then to the kids. They turned, looked at me, and then walked out. I followed them out, but by the time I got out the door, they had all got into the car. The entrance to the parking lot was blocked, so he started circling to find a way out, like a mouse in a maze. Why would they go to such lengths to make sure I wouldn't talk to Aden or Jaeda? I wondered. But that's the crazy part about dreams—they have the ability to manifest in the real world. If I had the ability to get close to my kids through a dream, what else could I achieve? All I wanted to do was say hi to the people I loved most in the world, to the people I had brought into the world. All I wanted to do was tell them I loved them.

My beautiful kids, I want you to know that you are what I am most thankful for. If I were given the choice to change anything in my life before I had you, I wouldn't change a thing. No matter what I have gone through, I would do it again because that path led me to having you. I understand what you are going through because I was in the exact fog you are in now. Once the fog clears and you realize the truth, I will be here with open arms ready to pick up where we left off, as if you were never gone—just like my parents did for me. As painful as it is to be rejected when I reach out to you, I will do it every chance I get, if for nothing else, so you will know I will always be here. I will gladly take that pain so you don't ever have the thought that your mom doesn't love you. There is no you without me, and there is no me without you. Our bond is everlasting. *I love you forever.*

ACKNOWLEDGMENTS

There are too many loved ones to thank for being there on this journey with me. First, Mom and Dad, I acknowledge your endless love and support. Thank you for showing me how to fight for what I love in this life. And my family, you know that it would take a whole book to thank each member. Thank you all for accepting me and making me feel safe and welcomed after choosing to leave and come back.

To Ashley, Blanca, and Dee, and my many friends, thank you all for being a shoulder to cry on, laugh, and battle this fight with me. Big thank you to my legacy family 169!

To my husband Steven, thank you for showing me what a healthy committed relationship can be. Thank you for allowing me to believe that love is possible.

Cory and Dwight, without you this book would not have been a reality. Thank you both for pushing me to get what's in my heart on to paper.

Most importantly, my children. Thank you for making me a mom and giving me the chance to know what true unconditional love is. No matter where you are in life, I will always love and fight for you. Looking forward to when we are united again.

ABOUT THE AUTHOR

Rosaline Alam is an author, mother, and parental alienation expert who writes to educate those experiencing alienation and to change the legal system. Rosaline currently lives in Southern California and spends her spare time traveling abroad, and of course, fighting to get her children back.

Rosaline has established the UNBREAKABLE BOND FOUNDATION to assist parents who are dealing with custody battles by providing training and supportive resources during their time of need through therapy, legal, and financial advice in hopes of preventing Parental Alienation and to preserve the bond between parent and child.

UNBREAKABLEBONDFOUNDATION.ORG